CONTENTS

CONTENTS

RECENT DEVELOPMENTS IN THE FEDERAL EMPLOYEES HEALTH BENEFITS PROGRAM

HEARING

BEFORE THE

SUBCOMMITTEE ON THE CIVIL SERVICE, CENSUS AND AGENCY ORGANIZATION

OF THE

COMMITTEE ON GOVERNMENT REFORM

HOUSE OF REPRESENTATIVES

ONE HUNDRED SEVENTH CONGRESS

SECOND SESSION

DECEMBER 11, 2002

Serial No. 107–221

Printed for the use of the Committee on Government Reform

Available via the World Wide Web: http://www.gpo.gov/congress/house
http://www.house.gov/reform

U.S. GOVERNMENT PRINTING OFFICE

87–416 PDF WASHINGTON : 2003

For sale by the Superintendent of Documents, U.S. Government Printing Office
Internet: bookstore.gpo.gov Phone: toll free (866) 512–1800; DC area (202) 512–1800
Fax: (202) 512–2250 Mail: Stop SSOP, Washington, DC 20402–0001

COMMITTEE ON GOVERNMENT REFORM

DAN BURTON, Indiana, *Chairman*

BENJAMIN A. GILMAN, New York
CONSTANCE A. MORELLA, Maryland
CHRISTOPHER SHAYS, Connecticut
ILEANA ROS-LEHTINEN, Florida
JOHN M. McHUGH, New York
STEPHEN HORN, California
JOHN L. MICA, Florida
THOMAS M. DAVIS, Virginia
MARK E. SOUDER, Indiana
STEVEN C. LATOURETTE, Ohio
BOB BARR, Georgia
DAN MILLER, Florida
DOUG OSE, California
RON LEWIS, Kentucky
JO ANN DAVIS, Virginia
TODD RUSSELL PLATTS, Pennsylvania
DAVE WELDON, Florida
CHRIS CANNON, Utah
ADAM H. PUTNAM, Florida
C.L. "BUTCH" OTTER, Idaho
EDWARD L. SCHROCK, Virginia
JOHN J. DUNCAN, JR., Tennessee
JOHN SULLIVAN, Oklahoma

HENRY A. WAXMAN, California
TOM LANTOS, California
MAJOR R. OWENS, New York
EDOLPHUS TOWNS, New York
PAUL E. KANJORSKI, Pennsylvania
PATSY T. MINK, Hawaii
CAROLYN B. MALONEY, New York
ELEANOR HOLMES NORTON, Washington, DC
ELIJAH E. CUMMINGS, Maryland
DENNIS J. KUCINICH, Ohio
ROD R. BLAGOJEVICH, Illinois
DANNY K. DAVIS, Illinois
JOHN F. TIERNEY, Massachusetts
JIM TURNER, Texas
THOMAS H. ALLEN, Maine
JANICE D. SCHAKOWSKY, Illinois
WM. LACY CLAY, Missouri
DIANE E. WATSON, California
STEPHEN F. LYNCH, Massachusetts

BERNARD SANDERS, Vermont (Independent)

KEVIN BINGER, *Staff Director*
DANIEL R. MOLL, *Deputy Staff Director*
JAMES C. WILSON, *Chief Counsel*
ROBERT A. BRIGGS, *Chief Clerk*
PHIL SCHILIRO, *Minority Staff Director*

SUBCOMMITTEE ON THE CIVIL SERVICE, CENSUS AND AGENCY ORGANIZATION

DAVE WELDON, Florida, *Chairman*

DAN MILLER, Florida
CONSTANCE A. MORELLA, Maryland
JOHN L. MICA, Florida
MARK E. SOUDER, Indiana
C.L. "BUTCH" OTTER, Idaho

DANNY K. DAVIS, Illinois
MAJOR R. OWENS, New York
ELEANOR HOLMES NORTON, Washington, DC
ELIJAH E. CUMMINGS, Maryland

EX OFFICIO

DAN BURTON, Indiana

HENRY A. WAXMAN, California

GARRY EWING, *Staff Director*
MARY BAGINSKY, *Professional Staff Member*
SCOTT SADLER, *Clerk*
TANIA SHAND, *Minority Professional Staff Member*

RECENT DEVELOPMENTS IN THE FEDERAL EMPLOYEES HEALTH BENEFITS PROGRAM

WEDNESDAY, DECEMBER 11, 2002

HOUSE OF REPRESENTATIVES,
SUBCOMMITTEE ON CIVIL SERVICE, CENSUS AND AGENCY ORGANIZATION,
COMMITTEE ON GOVERNMENT REFORM,
Washington, DC.

The subcommittee met, pursuant to notice, at 11:05 a.m., in room 2247, Rayburn House Office Building, Hon. Dave Weldon (chairman of the subcommittee) presiding.

Present: Representatives Weldon, Davis of Illinois, and Norton.

Also present: Representative Tom Davis of Virginia.

Staff present: Gary Ewing, staff director; Jim Lester, counsel; Scott Sadler, clerk; Mary Baginsky, professional staff member; Tania Shand, minority professional staff member; and Teresa Coufal, minority staff assistant.

Mr. WELDON. Good morning. I want to welcome everyone to this hearing on the Federal Employees Health Benefits Program.

During the past year there have been important developments in the FEHBP that are of interest to the subcommittee. The FEHBP is one of the most important programs this subcommittee oversees. In fact, Federal employees, retirees, and their families enjoy the widest selection of health plans in the country. This year they may choose from 188 plans. Because these choices are available, FEHBP participants may compare the costs, benefits and features of different plans to make an informed choice.

As a physician and the Representative of Florida's 15th District, I am keenly aware of the importance of the FEHBP. Over 8 million Federal employees, retirees, and dependents rely on the program for high quality health care options at affordable prices. I share their concerns about the program and look forward to the 108th Congress as an opportunity to improve competition and encourage innovation in the program.

I have spoken before about the need for innovation in the FEHBP. In that context, I want to commend the Office of Personnel Management and the American Postal Workers Union. Unlike the past years, OPM's call letter for 2003, which outlines OPM's program guidance for carriers, was not studded with new mandates. Indeed, OPM challenged carriers to be innovative.

The American Postal Workers Union accepted that challenge and developed its new consumer-driven option plan. The new consumer-driven option plan is unlike any other plan currently offered to Federal workers and retirees. The plan gives its members more control over their health care and provides incentives for them to be wise consumers of health care. It provides first dollar coverage through personal care accounts. If the personal care account is exhausted, there is a reasonable deductible before traditional health care insurance begins. A major advantage of these accounts is that they roll over year-to-year for up to 4 years, so members can save for unforeseen medical expenses.

OPM has approved another new and innovative option, flexible spending accounts, which will hopefully be available to FEHBP members in the summer of 2003. Under this program participants may set aside tax-free dollars from their paycheck to pay for certain health care costs.

Another important development that we saw this past September was the continuation of rising premiums for 2003. According to the Office of Personnel Management, on average, premiums will rise by 11.1 percent. These continuing increases are a cause of concern for participants and members alike—Members of Congress as well.

To put this increase in context, though, it is estimated that health care premiums in the United States could climb by an average of 15 percent this year. These increases reflect cost drivers such as increased utilization of prescription drugs, an aging population, advanced medical technology, and hospital costs and consolidation. CALPERS, California Public Employees' Retirement System, which provides retirement and health benefits and which many consider an exemplary program, will experience a 25 percent rate increase for 2003.

In another important development, the program's most popular carrier, Blue Cross/Blue Shield, nearly was forced to withdraw from the FEHBP after the House voted to end an exemption from cost accounting standards that carriers have enjoyed since 1998. Fortunately, OPM granted an administrative exemption to the accounting standards that made it possible for the Blues to remain in FEHBP.

Nevertheless, I remain concerned about this issue. It would be a tragedy if the most popular carrier in the program, especially one that so many of our retirees have chosen, were driven from the program by bureaucratic insistence on imposing a one-size-fits-all accounting system that would provide not one whit of benefits for those who participate in the plan or the taxpayer. Therefore, I believe this next Congress should seriously consider a permanent statutory exemption.

I look to our witnesses today for their perspectives on these important developments, and I know this subcommittee is interested in any recommendations they may have for ways to improve the program while preserving competition and consumer choice. Market orientation and consumer choice have been hallmarks of the program's success. These key features have made the FEHBP a widely admired model for employer-sponsored health care programs.

I look forward to hearing the testimony of our distinguished witnesses today, and I thank them for appearing.

And I now yield to the gentleman from Illinois, Mr. Davis, for his opening statement.

Mr. DAVIS OF ILLINOIS. Thank you very much, Mr. Chairman. And, first of all, let me just say that it has been a pleasure working with you during this past year, and I look forward to a delightful year coming. I also want to take this opportunity to wish and you and your family a happy, healthy and peaceful holiday season as well as for those who are assembled.

I want to thank you for scheduling this hearing. I want to thank all of the witnesses including the distinguished whip of the Democratic Caucus for being with us to testify.

Last year the Democratic members of the subcommittee requested this hearing to give witnesses with varying views on medical saving accounts and ideas of how best to reduce the FEHBP premiums an opportunity to testify before the subcommittee.

I also may indicate, Mr. Chairman, that this obviously would be one of the hardest working subcommittees. We may very well be the only committee that's holding a hearing at this particular moment and certainly the only one that's well attended. Though a year later, this hearing is taking place when there are many new developments in the Federal Employees Health Benefits premiums, and today's witnesses do indeed have varying opinions on how these developments will affect the FEHBP.

Earlier this year, the Office of Personnel Management announced that the FEHBP premiums for 2003 will increase an average of 11.1 percent. This increase marks the third consecutive year that premiums have jumped by more than 10 percent. Representative Steny Hoyer—who, I am pleased to say, will be testifying on our first panel—introduced H.R. 1307, which would help keep Federal employees' health care costs affordable by increasing the government's contribution to premiums. The bill would increase the government's share of the FEHBP premiums from 72 percent to 80 percent. This subcommittee should give this bill serious consideration next year, particularly since a million Federal employees will see their pay fall below that of their military counterparts.

OPM also announced that for the first time executive and legislative branch employees will be offered flexible spending accounts which allow a pretax payroll deduction for some insurance premiums, unreimbursed medical expenses, and child care and dependent care expenses. Additionally, beginning in 2003, the American Postal Workers Union, the APWU, will offer a new consumer-driven option to FEHBP participants. Consumer-driven plans are used to give employees more incentive to control the cost of their health benefits and to reduce employee spending on health care.

A report entitled "Can Consumerism Slow the Rate of Health Benefit Cost Increases," by Paul Fronstin with the Employee Benefit Research Institute, a nonprofit, nonpartisan organization, stated, "A movement to consumer-driven health benefits has implications for health benefit costs, utilization of health care services, quality of health care, the health status of the population, risk selection, and efforts to expand health insurance coverage. Ultimately the success or failure of consumer-driven health benefits will be measured by its effect on the cost of providing health benefits and its effect on the number of people with and without health benefits. Time will tell what impact the new consumer-driven plan, flexible spending accounts, and other new developments will have on premium increases and the quality of health care in the FEHBP."

I expect today's witnesses will help shed some light on what is ultimately coming in FEHBP and how they believe it will affect plan participants.

I request also, Mr. Chairman, that the record be kept open for 2 weeks so that Professor James Bedingfield, a member of the Cost Accounting Standards Board, can submit a statement for the record.

I thank you for this consideration and yield back the balance of my time.

[The prepared statement of Hon. Danny K. Davis follows:]

STATEMENT OF CONGRESSMAN DANNY K. DAVIS AT

A CIVIL SERVICE, CENSUS AND AGENCY ORGANIZATION SUBCOMMITTEE

HEARING

ON RECENT DEVELOPMENTS IN THE FEDERAL EMPLOYEE HEALTH BENEFITS PROGRAM

Wednesday, December 11, 2002

Mr. Chairman, I thank you for scheduling this hearing on the Federal Employee Health Benefits Program (FEHBP). Last year, the Democratic members of the subcommittee requested this hearing to give witnesses with varying views on medical savings accounts and ideas on how best to reduce FEHBP premiums, an opportunity to testify before the subcommittee.

Though a year later, this hearing is taking place when there are many new developments in FEHBP and today's witnesses, do indeed, have varying opinions on how these developments will affect FEHBP.

Earlier this year, the Office of Personnel Management (OPM) announced that FEHBP premiums for 2003 will increase an average of 11.1%. The increase marks the third consecutive year that premiums have jumped by more than 10%. Rep. Steny Hoyer, who I am pleased to say will be testifying on our first panel, introduced H.R. 1307 which would help keep federal employees health care costs affordable by increasing the Government's contribution to premiums. The bill would increase the government's share of FEHBP premiums from 72% to 80%. This subcommittee should give this bill serious consideration next session, particularly since civilian federal employees will see their pay fall below that of their military counterparts.

OPM also announced that, for the first time, executive and legislative branch employees will be offered flexible spending accounts, which allow a pretax payroll deduction for some insurance premiums, unreimbursed medical expenses and child care and dependent care expenses. Additionally, beginning in 2003, the American Postal Workers Union (APWU), will offer a new Consumer-driven option to FEHBP participants.

Consumer-driven plans are used to give employees more incentive to control the cost of their health benefits and to reduce employer spending on health care.

A report entitled, "Can "Consumerism" Slow the Rate of Health Benefit Cost Increases?" by Paul Fronstin with the Employee Benefit Research Institute, a non-profit, non-partisan organization, stated, "A movement to consumer-driven health benefits has implications for health benefit costs, utilization of health care services, quality of health care, the health status of the population, risk selection, and efforts to expand health insurance coverage. Ultimately, the success or failure of consumer-driven health benefits will be measured by its effect on the cost of providing health benefits and its effect on the number of people with and without health benefits."

Time will tell what impact the new consumer-driven plan, flexible spending accounts, and other new developments will have on premium increases and the quality of health care in FEHBP.

I expect today's witnesses will help shed some light on what is up and coming in FEHBP and how they believe it will affect plan participants.

I request that the record be kept open for two weeks so Professor James Bedingfield, a member of the Cost Accounting Standards Board, can submit a statement for the record.

Thank you.

Mr. WELDON. I thank the gentleman for his very kind words. And let me just add that it's been a pleasure to work with you for the past—I guess it's about 18 months—and I am looking forward to working with you and your staff in the future. And certainly I wish you, as well as your family, a pleasant holiday.

And without objection we will keep the record open for 2 weeks to allow for the testimony that you are speaking of.

Our first panel today, we have the distinguished Member from the State of Maryland, Mr. Steny Hoyer. Steny represents the Fifth District in Maryland, which is home to thousands of Federal employees and retirees, both military and civilian. Mr. Hoyer just completed his tenth full term, making him the longest serving Member of the U.S. House of Representatives from southern Maryland in history. For over two decades Mr. Hoyer has been very active in working on issues affecting Federal employees.

I want to commend Mr. Hoyer for his commitment to the Federal employees, and I want to congratulate him on his recent election as minority whip. And I want to thank him for testifying, and I look forward to hearing his views.

Without objection, your written statement will be entered into the record. And, Steny, you are recognized for your opening statement.

STATEMENT OF HON. STENY HOYER, A REPRESENTATIVE IN CONGRESS FROM THE STATE OF MARYLAND

Mr. HOYER. Thank you very much, Mr. Chairman.

And, Mr. Davis, I want to thank you for your comments and for your cosponsorship of the legislation to which you referred.

I also want to say to you, Mr. Chairman, I appreciated the opportunity to work with you on issues of relevance to Federal employees. You undertook this relatively new responsibility, and you have undertaken it, I think, with a great deal of ability and openness; and I appreciate the opportunity to work with you.

I want to thank you also for inviting me here to testify. The purpose of this hearing is to discuss recent developments in the Federal Employee Health Benefits Program, and I appreciate the opportunity to discuss a few of them with you and the committee today.

Specifically, I'd like to discuss first of all the affordability of the Federal Employee Health Benefits package, H.R. 1307, legislation to increase the Government's contribution for health premiums, premium conversion, flexible spending accounts and consumer-driven plans, all of which you've referred to. Let me say parenthetically, Mr. Chairman, that I served on the post office, civil service committee for 18 months. That committee no longer exists and essentially this subcommittee has undertaken its responsibilities. But a study was done in the mid-1980's about the relative worth of health benefit programs in the private sector, in the non-Federal public sector, and in the Federal sector, and that study, interestingly enough, showed that the Federal sector was the least generous of the health benefit plans that existed at that point in time.

A stark example of that was, I did not participate in the Federal Employee Health Benefit Plan until just a few years ago because my wife was an employee of the Prince George's County board of education, and the board of education plan was about as expensive, a little less expensive, but included dental benefits and it included a broader spectrum of benefits than was available under the Federal Health Benefit program. So that study that showed municipal and State plans to be more generous, as well as private-sector plans to be more generous, was very real for me because I found that out.

However, very frankly, over the last 15 years or so that situation has changed. It has changed in large part because, as health care costs have escalated, private-sector and State and municipal plans, not always but sometimes, have increasingly diminished the options available to employees and have increasingly provided as the only option a health maintenance organization, clearly directed at trying to minimize costs.

Since 1998, the FEHBP premiums have increased by nearly 50 percent, not including the average 11 percent jump scheduled for January 2003. Over the same period, salaries for Federal employees have increased by less than 15 percent. While those percentages are different bases, the fact of the matter is that every year participants of the health benefit program are digging deeper and deeper into their pockets to pay for their health care and thereby diminishing their take-home pay. For a Federal employee choosing Blue Cross/Blue Shield's basic family option, he or she pays over $2,000 per year in premium costs alone. Those making $30,000 to $40,000 a year are simply priced out of receiving coverage from Blue Cross/Blue Shield.

The rising costs of health care premiums is becoming a liability in retaining hard-working Federal employees, as well as recruiting those who are considering careers in public service. That liability is magnified when you consider that the Bureau of Labor Statistics estimates that Federal employees are paid 33 percent less than their private-sector counterparts, and although that is controversial and not universally accepted, particularly by OMB of both parties on a consistent basis, nevertheless there is no doubt that the percentage is a very substantial one. Nobody denies that.

Let me speak to the specific legislation that I have introduced with Congressman Davis and Congresswoman Morella and others. When the 107th Congress began, I introduced a bill to increase the Federal Government's premiums an average of 72 percent. Mr. Chairman, as you know, it is not specifically 72 percent; it is an average of 72 percent, not more than 75. By increasing it to 80 percent, it would bring the share of the Federal Government pay more in line with most private and State employee pay.

Hark back to the 1980's study, which Kaiser Permanente currently says is approximately 83.1 percent, on average, of the employers' contribution, private sector and public sector, non-Federal, which is—83, that's for single health care coverage. For a family, it is 76.2 percent, so that the 80 percent would be approximately an average of what the private sector and non-Federal public sector is doing.

There are now 250,000 Federal employees that choose not to enroll in the FEHBP; therefore, we should be focusing on reducing that number by making quality health care coverage available to all of our employees, as well as retirees. I plan to reintroduce this legislation when the 108th Congress convenes, and hope that this subcommittee, Mr. Chairman, will give it an early hearing.

Briefly, on premium conversion, in October 2000 Federal employees were offered what is called "premium conversion" as you have spoken about in your opening statement. In the midst of rising health care costs, premium conversion has become a significant benefit for participants in the FEHBP because costs for premiums, of course, come out of pretax dollars, saving participants an average of $450 annually, a very significant benefit. This is a long overdue benefit, which is similar to most private-sector plans which have allowed their employees to deduct health insurance premiums from their taxable incomes for many, many years.

Unfortunately, the Federal Government does not offer the same benefit to retired Federal employees. H.R. 2125, the bill sponsored by Representative Tom Davis, and which I have cosponsored—and I think there are 200-plus cosponsors on it, well over a majority—will allow Federal retirees to use pretax earnings to pay their health insurance premiums. I would hope the committee will also hold a hearing on that piece of legislation.

Flexible spending accounts: In the spirit of premium conversion, I am pleased to see that OPM plans to proceed with flexible spending accounts in 2003. FSAs will allow Federal employees to contribute to a personal account out of pretaxed dollars which they can later tap to pay for uncovered portions of qualified medical costs and other expenses. However, to make these accounts work most effectively, I would like to see Congress consider the President's fiscal year 2003 budget proposal to allow up to $500 in remaining balances to be carried over. This would provide employees in the public and private sector much-needed flexibility.

Last, consumer-driven plans: As the committee knows, the American Postal Workers Union is now offering a new consumer-driven option in the FEHBP. This plan allows participants to receive a health-spending account which you referred to, Mr. Chairman, and Mr. Davis did as well. Employees will be able to draw from the account to pay for a variety of medical needs. While this new option may keep costs down, the Federal Government should proceed slowly, in my opinion, on these types of plans; not all participants, possibly, will benefit from the plan.

But I think the experiment is a very worthwhile one and that we ought to watch closely. While a healthier person will benefit, those with greater health care needs could end up paying higher premium costs down the road. I know the National Association of Retired Federal Employees is opposed to this plan, and President Charles Fallis will be addressing the problems in depth later today.

I hope the APWU plan is not a prelude to a more comprehensive medical savings account. I know that has been discussed and some of us have great reservations for medical savings accounts because we believe, as we referred to them, the healthy and wealthy will be advantaged by such plans. But because you would take the healthy and wealthy out of the insurance pool into savings accounts, you will increase the risk in the remainder and premiums and costs will go up in the remaining pool.

When the Office of Personnel Management Deputy Director Dan Blair testified before the Treasury, Postal Appropriations Subcommittee, of which I am the ranking member, I asked him if the administration was pursuing medical savings accounts as a policy. His answer was that MSAs were, in fact, being considered.

Let me conclude Mr. Chairman, with a word of caution on MSAs which frankly I have already given so I will not repeat it because my time is up, but I would hope that as that is considered, this committee would look very carefully at the impact that proposal would have on the insurance pool and the consequential increase in premiums of the remainder.

Thank you, Mr. Chairman. Again, I appreciate this opportunity and hope that the committee will seriously consider increasing the premium contribution that the Federal Government makes. This is a bipartisan piece of legislation reflecting the employer's efforts to keep employees insured and whole in terms of salary increases.

Mr. WELDON. I want to thank the gentleman for his testimony.

Your comments about taking your wife's insurance plan reminded me that my parents did the same thing. My father was a postal worker, my mother was a school teacher, but the family was on my mother's plan rather than my father's plan because it was more generous.

Mr. HOYER. I was surprised—I think it was the Hudson Institute that ran the study in the mid-1980's for the post office, civil service committee, and frankly I wasn't on the civil service committee at that point in time. But I was very interested, as you pointed out, because I have a lot of Federal employees. But I was surprised at the disparity between both the private-sector and municipal and State plans.

Mr. WELDON. It would be interesting to repeat that study today, and I agree with your assessment. I would conjecture that the gap is not nearly as it has been in the past——

Mr. HOYER. I haven't seen the study, but that is my belief because of the fact, as I said, the private-sector plans and municipal plans have become less generous because of the increasing costs.

Mr. WELDON. Your piece of legislation is—your 1307 that you plan to reintroduce, have you had it scored by CBO as yet?

Mr. HOYER. We have not, Mr. Chairman, but it is my belief, and just from speculating on what the costs would be as it relates to the existing costs at 72 percent, that we are talking probably at least a couple hundred million dollars a year.

Mr. WELDON. We did some back-of-the envelope calculations, and the mandatory spending increase would be on the order of several hundred million dollars a year. So it would be helpful to try to come up with some offsets if we are going to try to pursue legislation like this.

Are you concerned at all about raising the government's share of the premiums serving as a disincentive for Federal employees to shop around for the best value?

Mr. HOYER. Mr. Chairman, I have been one who has supported the concept of deductibles and the concept of participation by the insured in the payment of the premium, as well as some of the costs of health care, to avoid overutilization and to encourage careful shopping. My view is that frankly the difference between 20 percent and 28 percent will not be a difference which will undermine the employees still wanting to save and get as good a buy from the 20 percent that they are contributing, particularly as costs go up.

I frankly don't perceive there to be a significant savings to the Federal employees by this. What I perceive it to be is a freezing of—in effect, going backward; so that my view is that if you went to 100 percent, or maybe 95 percent or even maybe 90 percent, that would be a greater problem than simply the increase of 8 points. But I don't think that will in any meaningful way affect the consumers' judgment.

Mr. WELDON. Like you, I am concerned about the impact of higher premiums on the work force. I held a hearing on cafeteria plans last March. Witnesses testified about the benefits those plans offer and said they helped employers recruit and retain well-qualified employees because they allow employees to maximize the value of benefits offered by the employer.

A cafeteria plan could be designed to allow employees to use the government contribution to pay for 100 percent of the FEHBP premium. Would you be willing to work with me on examining cafeteria plans for Federal employees?

Mr. HOYER. Mr. Chairman, the answer is, I would certainly be willing to work with you. I will be candid in saying that I have had grave reservations about cafeteria plans. I am not an expert on the cafeteria plans, particularly as they apply in the private sector, but I am very worried that cafeteria plans will adversely affect senior employees in particular, people who have been here for some period of time.

Newer employees, who have less expense, particularly in the health care area, may find them to be more advantageous than more senior employees. But the answer to your question is, I would certainly look at them with you because obviously in the private sector they are being utilized; and there's a lot of discussion about applying them in the public sector, but up to this point in time, I haven't been very enthusiastic about that option.

Mr. WELDON. I agree with you that Congress should seriously consider the President's proposal to allow employees to roll over up to $500 in their flexible spending accounts. According to many experts, the use-it-or-lose-it feature of flexible spending accounts deters many employees, particularly lower-income employees, from taking advantage of FSAs.

Permitting rollover would also discourage wasteful end-of-the-year spending.

Do you think we can work together on this issue in the next Congress?

Mr. HOYER. Certainly. I look forward to it.

Mr. WELDON. Some experts have suggested that even without a cafeteria plan, Congress should eliminate the statutory requirement that employees pay at least 25 percent of the FEHBP premium. They say it is a disincentive for employees and retirees to shop for the best value and that employees and retirees should be able to use the government contribution to pay for 100 percent of premiums.

Is this something you think the subcommittee should be examining in the future?

Mr. HOYER. Well, as I said, I tend to adopt the premise that a copay plan probably focuses the purchaser, which is the employee, notwithstanding the fact that there is either 72 percent, or in my proposal 80 percent, contribution by the Federal Government; and it focuses the purchaser on making the best buy because they are in fact expending some of their funds. If you, obviously, give the option of 100 percent pay, that undermines that.

On the other hand, as health care costs escalate, there may well be families, particularly at the lower level of pay, that would be costed out of the market without 100 percent contribution. So I think we ought to look at it in terms of affordability of health care.

Frankly, at our level of pay, it really is not a major issue for us. But at a GS–3, GS–4, GS–5, GS–6, GS–7, with a family, it is a major, major issue, and we ought to look at it in that context.

Mr. WELDON. I was thinking of it not so much in the context of copays, but more in premiums; and it is somewhat in line with the objectives——

Mr. HOYER. I'm sorry, you're talking about 100 percent payment of premiums?

Mr. WELDON. Yes.

Mr. HOYER. Yes. And my point is, to go back to your question, if you pay 100 percent of premiums, does the purchaser therefore not try to make the best buy for it in this—and we have 100-some odd alternatives. Obviously, as you well know, all of those aren't available to all Federal employees; it is a regional thing, and that is the total number of plans that are available throughout the country.

I think in this area—does anybody know? We have maybe 25, 30—25 or 30 if you are an employee in the Washington metropolitan area; Chicago, I don't know how many; or in Florida, central Florida, I'm not sure.

But in any event, I was responding to your concept that can apply both to copays and to premium payment because the initial amount of premium does, in fact, determine for an employee what policy they are going to be able to afford, what policy is best for them and their families that is affordable by them. That was my point in terms of saying, obviously the less you're paid, the more critical becomes the contribution the Federal Government makes, the employer makes, to the purchase. The lower the employee, the closer I think we ought to get to 100 percent. That is not what we do now because as we do it at every level, an average of 72 percent.

Mr. WELDON. I believe my time has expired, and I would love to explore this more with you. And it is a pleasure to recognize the ranking member for questions.

Mr. DAVIS OF ILLINOIS. Thank you very much, Mr. Chairman.

It was very interesting to hear both you and Mr. Hoyer relate experiences that you had with spouses who work for the board of education and were members of the teachers union. I have a very similar experience—that is, when my wife used to work.

Mr. WELDON. I feel your pain.

Mr. HOYER. Let me say on behalf of all the wives that aren't getting salaries, they work.

Mr. DAVIS OF ILLINOIS. They still work. But my question really becomes, it looks like they have done pretty good jobs of negotiating benefits packages in their contracts.

Do you feel that OPM has done a competent job, or a good job, of negotiating coverage for the Federal employees at the best possible cost?

Mr. HOYER. Really I don't think the Congressman could say that they have done the best job, but clearly if you look at the disparity between the private-sector escalation and the FEHBP escalation, there is about a 25 percent better buy for the Federal employee. That would appear to say that we have done a good job.

On the other hand, it would also be reflective of the fact that we have approximately 9 million people who are involved in this program between active Federal employees, dependents, and retirees. That is a big cohort, so we have a lot of leverage in negotiation. So it may simply reflect the savings that we effect from having a large number of purchasers.

On the other hand, I think it would be fair to say that I think OPM has been pretty vigorous in trying to negotiate well on behalf of Federal employees.

Let me say in passing, I don't want to get in trouble with Mr. Weldon. I don't know his position on this, so I have sort of a gut feeling. But essentially what the Clinton health care plan recommended in many respects was a replication of FEHBP with, in effect, the States serving as OPM and managing the market competition with individuals within States buying, as they do for FEHBP, from private-sector insurers. I think they didn't sell it very well, and it wasn't understood that simply, but in some respects that's what they were saying.

Obviously, that didn't go very well. Harry and Louise took care of that. But my answer would be, it is hard for me to judge, had they done the best job they could have? Clearly, given the bulk of our purchase and the negotiations that we involve ourselves in, I think we are getting a pretty good deal.

Mr. DAVIS OF ILLINOIS. And I would be in agreement with that. Of course, some of the concern that has been expressed is that, in fact, it is kind of difficult for OPM to take the same position, let us say, a union might take on behalf of its membership and therein might be a little bit of the difference in terms of the kind of agreements that ultimately may have gotten reached with some of the teachers unions, some of the other entities that have had to negotiate contracts; and I certainly agree with your thinking there.

But you mentioned that there were 250,000 Federal employees who choose not to enroll in the Federal package, and you also mentioned that the rising cost of health premiums is becoming a liability to the extent that, in some instances, it prevents us from being able to recruit and maintain the kind of work force that we need.

Can you think of any examples of areas where this might prove true?

Mr. HOYER. I don't have a specific example, Congressman, but clearly, as I said, the Kaiser Permanente figure is about 83 percent in the private sector for a single insured and 76 percent for family policies. If that is the case, if an individual seeks employment at the Federal level and sees a disparity, an 11 percent difference, 72 to 83, 11 percent difference on what their health premium will pay, I think for younger workers it probably won't make any difference. Younger workers for the most part are not driven in terms of their employment decision by health care benefits and probably not by retirement benefits either, but mid-level—recruiting mid-level people, skilled people who may be in their late 30's, early 40's, they have a family, children, children in their teens; they are starting to think of that. And although I don't have a specific example for you, we are going to be, as you know, faced in the next 6 years with approximately half of the Federal employees that we have, having the ability to retire.

Now, if that is the case, we won't be able to replace them all with young workers. We will have to replace some of them with experienced, skilled workers to replace the skills that we are going to lose at that point in time; and at that point in time, I think this will become a very important, competitive question as it relates to employment.

Mr. DAVIS OF ILLINOIS. Mr. Chairman, I know that my time is up, but with your indulgence, can I just get one additional question?

Mr. WELDON. Without objection.

Mr. DAVIS OF ILLINOIS. Have you received any outright opposition to 1307 in terms of anybody that has just said they are opposed to it, and what is your feeling about prognosis? I know you have indicated that you hope the committee would take a good look at it at the beginning of the year. But what is your prognosis in terms of movement of it?

Mr. HOYER. Congressman, as I told you and as you know very well and as Chairman Weldon knows, this is a bipartisan piece of legislation. This is not—this is a judgment call that we need to make as the employer, and that judgment call is, how much do we contribute to make us competitive and to assure that our employees have affordable health care for themselves and their families? I think as a model employer, that is very basic. We want that for every employee, but certainly we want it for our employees.

Mr. Weldon raised the point of several hundred million dollars, a point—and I think we are going to do 4.1 percent, by the way; I hope you will support that. Speaker Hastert is supporting 4.1 percent. I think when we come back we are going to do 4.1 percent.

The President did 3.1 percent under the law. I think he just followed the law and did that. And I think we will do the 4.1 percent. Having said that, that clearly would be offset by the premium increase. So we are going to keep Federal employees relatively even.

Let us say for the sake of argument, it is $250 million. One point is about $900 million. So we are talking about a quarter of a point on salary. So when you say on an offset, Mr. Chairman, obviously the employer's income, whatever you do, including the doctor's office, a law office, you have to consider, first of all, how do I pay my people because that is the critical component of the service organizations that they are involved in, and the Federal Government is obviously people-driven in terms of its expenses.

I think $250 million or thereabouts is a relatively small cost when you consider the $2 trillion budget for assuring affordable availability of health care for our employees and to put us in a competitive position. So I don't think it is a question of offsets. It is a question of dedicating your resources and whatever other incremental increases we will have next year. Obviously our revenue will go up, our taxes, and hopefully will produce more as the economy comes back. I think it is a justifiable cost we ought to spend, and I have not heard of any opposition to it, but there will obviously be concern about costs, as there ought to be.

Mr. DAVIS OF ILLINOIS. Thank you.

Thank you, Mr. Chairman.

Mr. WELDON. I want to thank Mr. Hoyer for his valuable testimony, and I assure you, we will take under consideration as we deliberate on these issues in the future. And I am certainly interested in trying to work with you on some of the issues that you raise in 1307. I think there may be a way for us to achieve both of our goals as we work on this issue in the future.

And with that, I will——

Mr. HOYER. I look forward to it.

Mr. WELDON. I will let you go ahead and proceed on. I know you have a busy schedule. It has been a pleasure to have you here.

Mr. HOYER. Thank you, Mr. Chairman. The witnesses—I have seen the list. The witnesses that will speak after me are much more knowledgeable.

Mr. WELDON. OK.

With that, I would like to now ask our second panel to come forward. But before I introduce them, we will proceed a little bit out of order here.

Mr. Davis wanted to say some words about one of the witnesses.

Mr. DAVIS OF VIRGINIA. On the third panel.

Mr. WELDON. On the third panel, OK.

STATEMENT OF HON. TOM DAVIS, A REPRESENTATIVE IN CONGRESS FROM THE STATE OF VIRGINIA

Mr. DAVIS OF VIRGINIA. Let me just say, Mr. Chairman, thanks. And let me first commend you for holding this hearing on a very important issue to me and tens of thousands of my constituents in northern Virginia on the Employees Health Benefits program. As you know, the FEHBP has become one of the most important pieces of the Federal employee benefit package. It plays a vital role in our recruitment and retention of good people in government, and it is of utmost importance that we all work together to ensure that quality and choice are maintained while we try to constrain costs.

But I thank you for the opportunity to introduce to the committee somebody who will be on the third panel, and I have to unfortunately go out to Loudoun County and speak to Federal Government employees out there.

But we have a newly elected president making his debut before this committee today, the new president of the National Association of Retired Federal Employees—Charles, do you want to get up—and I introduce him to the panel. He just began his term as the NARFE president on November 1, after having served two terms as the national treasurer. He is a Virginian. He was in various leadership posts in the Roanoke Chapter and in the Virginia Federation of Chapters.

Let me just note that he began his 35 years in the Federal civilian service as a substitute railway mail clerk, PFS level–5, rising through the agency ranks to postal inspector, schemes and routing officer, district manager for Virginia, officer in charge of Washington, DC, and the director of regional operations in the Eastern Region. In 1972, he was promoted into management with the rank of regional assistant postmaster general, Eastern Region, which includes the States of New York, Pennsylvania, New Jersey, Delaware, Maryland, Virginia, West Virginia, and the District.

Charlie's history of government service, I think, and his many years as an active member and elected leader of NARFE makes him an excellent source of information and assistance to this committee, as it has been to me for many years. And his honesty, his trustworthiness and thoroughness are well known to those of us who have known him for years; and I think it will be beneficial to the subcommittee's work, as we try to provide the best for those who serve our Nation as members of the Federal civil service.

And Charles, I apologize, I will not be here to hear your testimony, but I've got your written remarks. They look great. You are on an outstanding panel with some of the veterans who have been before this committee before, and we welcome you to the brotherhood, those of us who are fighting for Federal employees. Thank you for being here.

And, Mr. Chairman, let me just thank you for letting me speak out of turn.

Mr. WELDON. Thank you, Mr. Davis. It is a pleasure to have you here.

[The prepared statement of Hon. Tom Davis follows:]

Introductory Statement by Representative Tom Davis
For
Mr. Charles Fallis, President, NARFE
U.S. House of Representatives Subcommittee on Civil Service
December 11, 2002

Good morning Mr. Chairman and Members of the Committee. I want to commend you for holding this hearing on the important issue of the Federal Employees Health Benefit Program. As you well know, the FEHBP has become one of the most important pieces of the federal employees benefit package, and plays a vital role in our recruitment and retention efforts. It is therefore of the utmost importance that we all work together to ensure that quality and choice are maintained while constraining cost.

I want to thank you for allowing me the opportunity to introduce to the Committee today, for the first time, the newly-elected President of the National Association of Retired Federal Employees, Mr. Charles Fallis. Mr. Fallis began his term as NARFE National President on November 1, having served two terms as National Treasurer and in various leadership posts in the Roanoke chapter and in the Virginia Federation of Chapters.

He began his 35 years in the federal civilian service as a substitute railway mail clerk PFS Level-5, rising through agency ranks to Postal Inspector,

Schemes and Routing Officer, District Manager for Virginia, Officer-in-Charge (Postmaster), Washington, DC and Director of Regional Operations, Eastern Region. In 1972 he was promoted into management with the rank of Regional Assistant Postmaster General (RAPMG), Eastern Region, which included the states of New York, Pennsylvania, New Jersey, Delaware, Maryland, Virginia, West Virginia and the District of Columbia.

Charlie's history of government service and many years as an active member and elected leader in NARFE have made him an excellent source of information and assistance to me through the years. His honesty, trustworthiness, and thoroughness are well-known and will be beneficial to the subcommittee's work of providing the best for those who serve our nation as members of the federal civil service.

Thank you.

Mr. WELDON. I would like to ask the Honorable Dan Blair to come forward. Mr. Blair is the deputy director of the U.S. Office of Personnel Management. Mr. Blair is no stranger to the Committee on Government Reform or to this subcommittee. He had a long and distinguished career on the House staff, including on the staff of the Government Reform Committee. He served as the staff director for the House Subcommittee on Postal Service.

Before assuming his current post, Mr. Blair served on the staff of the Senate Committee on Governmental Affairs, where he helped develop a long-term care insurance program for Federal employees and the uniformed services, and reforms for the Federal Employees Health Benefits program and life insurance programs.

I want to thank you for being here, and as I see, you are accompanied by Mr. Ed Flynn who—it is a pleasure to have him, as well, and he will be available for responding to questions, but does not have a opening statement.

It is the practice of the Government Reform Committee to swear in witnesses at all of our hearings. I ask that you rise and raise your right hand.

[Witnesses sworn.]

Mr. WELDON. The court reporter will note that they answered in the affirmative. You are now recognized for your opening statement, Mr. Blair.

STATEMENT OF DAN BLAIR, DEPUTY DIRECTOR, U.S. OFFICE OF PERSONNEL MANAGEMENT, ACCOMPANIED BY ED FLYNN, SENIOR POLICY ADVISOR TO THE DIRECTOR

Mr. BLAIR. Good morning, Mr. Chairman, Congressman Davis. Thank you for that kind introduction. I am accompanied today by Ed Flynn, who is Director James's senior policy advisor.

You have a copy of my prepared testimony before you, and in the interest of time, I ask that my complete statement be entered for the record and I will be happy to summarize.

Director James asked me to testify for her today before this distinguished subcommittee on developments in the Federal Employee Health Benefits Program over the past year. I would like to tell you about her four-point strategy to maintain quality, to constrain costs in the program, and discuss the future direction of the program in the fifth pillar that she has added to her results-oriented strategy for the coming year.

Last March Director James spoke to the FEHBP plan carriers, and she warned them that OPM was going to be a tough and demanding negotiating partner. She challenged them to bring us their best and most innovative proposals. She directed OPM staff to negotiate hard for quality coverage at the best possible rate.

She also initiated a comprehensive outside audit to review mandates affecting participating plans over the past decade and maintained a close and ongoing relationship with OPM's Office of Inspector General in support of their joint efforts to cultivate a culture of accountability at all levels within the program.

Like all other purchasers, we saw continued premium increases for 2003. We were able to announce an overall average increase of 11.1 percent, more than 2 percentage points better than last year's 13.3 percent increase and well below estimated national trends.

CALPERS, the second largest employer-purchaser in the country and, as you referenced in your opening statement, sir, announced a rate increase of up to 25 percent for 2003.

Keeping our program increases to the lowest possible translates to tangible dividends of almost $1 billion, and these results are directly attributable to the Director's strategy.

Another factor in the program's favorable pay rate increase is choice. We don't micromanage the health care plans. We encourage and support the creativity and ingenuity of the private sector. Giving members a choice of plans promotes healthy competition, helps contain costs, and enhances the quality of services. We offer greater choice and variety than almost any other employer, 188 health plan options for 2003. All enrollees will have at least a dozen nationwide fee-for-service options in addition to local HMOs.

Among the options available to enrollees is the new consumer-driven Standard Option introduced by the American Postal Workers Union. It is representative of the innovation that Director James talked about and invited from carriers and trends in the industry as a whole. We believe this is a very promising approach, one which may help to hold down health care costs by giving consumers additional control, as well as an increased awareness of how they spend their health care dollars.

In addition to concerns about the magnitude of premium increases, we face another hurdle for 2003. As a result of action taken by the House that deleted from our appropriations bill language that waived application of the cost accounting standards to FEHBP contracts, Director James had to make a crucial decision. In September, she used the administrative process authorized for her use under the National Defense Authorization Act for fiscal year 2000 to waive the application of the CAS for all experience-rated carriers in the program. She acted to ensure that we could conduct an orderly and timely open season and that members would not face uncertainty about any plans' participations in the program for the coming year.

She also acted with the knowledge that adequate financial safeguards are already in place to protect taxpayer and member dollars. By acting promptly, she was able to preserve choice for members while maintaining fiscal accountability for health plans. Director James firmly believes that her action was in the best interests of the FEHBP program and the more than 8 million employees, retirees, and family members who depend on it for their health care coverage.

I'm also pleased to report progress toward implementation of the valuable addition to the Federal benefits package that will reduce out-of pocket costs for Federal employees. That's the implementation of flexible spending accounts. OPM has issued a request for a proposal for a third-party administrator this fall. Bids are coming in this week. We expect the first open season to begin in May and both health care and dependent care accounts to be available in July 2003. After that, the FSA sign-up season will be aligned with the health care open season.

We will continue to work with other government agencies, as well as private-sector and nonprofit organizations, to enhance patient safety, improve quality and accountability, and constrain costs in the health care system. OPM will strengthen these efforts with the addition of greatly enhanced consumer education in the coming year. We will work internally and with health plans to make sure that the consumers we serve have the information they need when they need it, that they understand it, and that they make choices based upon it. The payoff for this effort will be enhanced quality, more appropriate utilization of services, and the adoption of healthy life-styles and health care choices that will preserve and enhance the health status of Federal employees, retirees, and their families.

Again, thank you for this chance to discuss the developments of the FEHBP program over the last year and to provide some insights into our plans for the year to come. I'm very proud of the steps we've taken, but because we recognize how important the program is to the government as it seeks to recruit and retain the work force we need to keep our country safe and secure, we must do more. Director James and I, and the OPM team, pledge to work even harder to maintain quality and to control costs. We are committed to collaborate with you and with our stakeholders to keep the program a model for employer-provided health care coverage.

This concludes my summarized statement, and I'm pleased to respond to any questions you or the other Members may have. Thank you.

[The prepared statement of Mr. Blair follows:]

STATEMENT OF
DAN G. BLAIR
DEPUTY DIRECTOR
OFFICE OF PERSONNEL MANAGEMENT

at an oversight hearing of the

SUBCOMMITTEE ON CIVIL SERVICE, CENSUS AND AGENCY ORGANIZATION
COMMITTEE ON GOVERNMENT REFORM
U. S. HOUSE OF REPRESENTATIVES

on

THE FEDERAL EMPLOYEES HEALTH BENEFITS PROGRAM

DECEMBER 11, 2002

Mr. Chairman and Members of the Subcommittee:

I want to thank you for the opportunity to be here today to discuss the Federal Employees Health Benefits Program. The program enrolls 2.1 million employees and 1.9 million retirees and survivors. Including family members, it provides benefits to over 8 million people and paid annual premiums to health plans in 2002 of over 24 billion dollars.

As this Subcommittee knows, the President has called upon agencies to become market-based and results-oriented, rather than process driven. The primary message to embrace from the President's Management Agenda and his Fiscal Year 2003 budget is that results are what matter in the end. The President's message presents an important challenge and opportunity for Federal agencies.

This morning, I would like to tell you about the four-point strategy developed by our Director, Kay Coles James, to achieve the results in the FEHB program: maintaining quality through competition while simultaneously constraining costs.

Last March, Director James spoke to the FEHB plan carriers and reminded them of President Bush's principles of patient-centered health care, preservation of choice, and excellent quality. She warned them that OPM was going to be a demanding partner and challenged them to bring us their best, most innovative proposals. Second, for the first time in OPM history, she met with and directed OPM staff to negotiate hard for quality coverage at the best possible rate. Third, she initiated a comprehensive outside audit to review mandates affecting participating plans over the past decade so we can inform the Congress and the FEHB population about the costs of mandated health care services. Fourth, complementing our negotiating strategy, she has maintained a close and ongoing relationship with the OPM Inspector General and has aggressively supported his efforts to detect and control fraud and cultivate a culture of accountability within the FEHB program at all levels – among health plans themselves, among Federal participants, and within OPM.

Rate Increases For 2003

The Director's four-point strategy is providing dividends, both to the taxpayer and to Federal participants. The plans submitted well thought out proposals for 2003, and the OPM team bargained hard as it worked through last summer's benefits and rate negotiations. While we must always be concerned about premium increases, we were able to announce an overall average FEHB premium increase of 11.1 percent for 2003, more than 2 percent better than last year's 13.3 percent increase and well below nationwide trends estimated to be averaging about 15 percent. CalPers, the second largest employer-purchaser in the country, announced rate increases of up to 25 percent for 2003. In the Washington area, Montgomery County raised its premiums by 26 percent. When you consider that every 1 percent increase in premiums costs the taxpayer and participants $240 million, I think you will agree that the Director's strategy paid tangible dividends for 2003. That 4 percent below nationwide premium trends translates into savings of almost a billion dollars. Furthermore, we accomplished this with very little in the way of benefit reductions.

Contributors To The Premium Increase

There are a number of reasons for rising premiums. In general, the Federal employee program rates reflect changes in the health care marketplace, and those costs are continuing to rise. Key factors include increases in both the cost and utilization of medical services and pharmaceuticals and an increasingly older population. The Director has tasked me with streamlining and improving the hiring process for Government, a critical requirement as we address the effects of an aging workforce. One result of this changing demographic, however, will also likely be a younger Federal workforce and may mitigate future premiums increases.

The Value Of Choice

In addition to the Director's initiatives to control costs and maintain quality which she announced as part of the 2003 program, an important factor in the program's favorable comparison with rate increases at the national level is choice. We do not micro-manage the health benefits program; we encourage and support the creativity and the ingenuity of the private sector. Giving members a choice of plans promotes healthy competition, helps contain costs, and enhances the quality of services.

The Federal Government offers its employees and retirees greater choice than almost any other employer – 188 health plan choices in 2003. All enrollees will have at least a dozen nationwide fee-for-service options in addition to local HMOs.

FEHB initiatives

For 2003, we challenged carriers to propose innovative ideas to contain costs, maintain quality and keep the program a model of consumer choice and on the cutting edge of employer-sponsored health benefits. The new consumer-driven standard option introduced by the American Postal Workers Union (APWU) is representative of the innovations that are occurring in the industry as a whole. APWU and the FEHB negotiating team worked tirelessly to make that effort a reality.

We believe this is a very promising approach, one which may help to hold down health care costs by giving consumers a little more control and increased awareness of how they are spending their health-care dollars.

The APWU plan will feature up-front personal care accounts. Members will be able to use their accounts to pay for co-payments, deductibles and other out-of-pocket costs, as well as some additional services – such as dental and vision care – that are often not covered or covered only minimally by traditional plans. Enrollees can draw from their personal care account as they have medical expenses. If they exceed the amount in their personal care account, they must pay a deductible before traditional fee-for-service health insurance coverage takes over. One important feature of the personal care account is that unspent dollars can be rolled over to the next year. We will be very interested to see how Federal employees and retirees react to this cutting-edge product offering.

Flexible Spending Accounts

I am also pleased to report progress toward the implementation of a valuable addition to the Federal benefits package that will reduce out-of-pocket costs for Federal employees — flexible spending accounts or FSAs. This is a logical next step to premium conversion which we implemented earlier.

Employees will be able to set up a health care FSA using pre-tax dollars. As with the APWU personal care accounts, funds in the FSA can be used for out-of-pocket health care costs expenses not covered or covered only minimally by insurance. Employees also will be able to set up an FSA account to cover dependent-care expenses for children and aging parents.

OPM issued a request for proposals for a third party administrator this fall. Bids are coming in this week. We expect the first open season to begin in May, and accounts to be available in July 2003. After that, the FSA sign-up season will be aligned with the FEHB program open season.

Cost Accounting Standards

In addition to concerns about the magnitude of premium increases, we faced another major challenge for 2003. As a result of action by the house that deleted from OPM's appropriations bill language that waived application of the cost accounting standards to FEHB contracts, Director James had to make a critical decision. In September, she used the administrative process under the national defense authorization act for FY 2000 to waive the application of the cost accounting standards (CAS) for all the affected experience-rated carriers in the program. she acted to ensure that we could conduct an orderly and timely open season and that members would not face uncertainty about any plan's participation in the program for the coming year. She also acted with the knowledge that adequate financial safeguards are already in place to protect taxpayer and member dollars.

Director James firmly believes that her action was in the best interest of the FEHB program and the more than eight million employees, retirees, and family members who depend upon it for their health insurance coverage.

Study On Mandated Benefits

For a number of years, observers of the Federal Employees Health Benefits program have held differing views on the impact of benefit mandates. While various internal analyses of this issue have been conducted, the effect of mandated benefits on FEHB premiums has never been fully analyzed by an outside party. Earlier this year, Director James initiated a comprehensive, retrospective independent study to review the costs of Federal and State mandates over the past decade so that we can tell Federal enrollees, the congress, and others the true cost of mandated services. We expect to see the results of the study by early next year once analysis is completed.

Quality Initiatives

OPM is involved in a variety of activities to ensure that the FEHB program is aligned with President Bush's principles of patient-centered health care, preservation of choice, and excellent quality.

Fraud And Abuse:

Early this year, working closely with the OPM inspector general, we are studying our fraud and abuse program to ensure that it is consistent with industry standards and providing effective prevention and detection. To support the culture of accountability within the program, we developed a four-point strategy to: 1) raise consumer awareness about fraud and abuse through expanded information in the FEHB guide and the plan brochures; 2) raise health plan awareness by listing best practices that plans should be implementing; 3) incorporate plan fraud and abuse reporting into the audit process; and 4) in collaboration with OPM's Office of Inspector General and others, hold health plans accountable for preventing, detecting, and controlling fraud.

We are working closely with the plans to ensure that their fraud and abuse programs meet our standards. We also are identifying innovative and effective approaches we can share with others.

Health Plan Quality and Patient Safety: we use a combination of recognized standard industry measures, such as surveys on patients' experience of care and data on health care processes and outcomes, to inform members so they can make educated choices about their health care coverage. We also require plans to report on the quality of their services to members in accordance with contractual quality assurance standards.

We expect all FEHB plans to encourage their providers to implement generally recognized patient safety measures and to inform their members of provider performance. For 2003, plans with independently accredited provider networks are annotating their provider directories to communicate that information to consumers. As new and generally accepted safety and quality standards are put in place, FEHB plans will make information available to their members about providers that report on their performance.

Finally, we continue to work with other Federal Government agencies, through the quality interagency coordination task force, and with private sector and nonprofit organizations, through the national quality forum and other organizations, to coordinate our work on quality improvement and accountability.

Future Direction: Consumer Education

While an 11.1 % average premium increase is small compared to industry trends, it is nevertheless significant and means employees and retirees, as well as the Government, will pay more for health insurance in 2003. Because we understand that we must continue to strengthen our efforts, Director James has added a fifth pillar to her results-oriented strategy for the coming year: consumer education.

OPM will work internally and with the health plans to make sure that the consumers we serve have the information they need when they need it, that they understand it and that they make choices based upon it. The payoff for this effort will be enhanced quality, more appropriate utilization of services, and adoption of healthy life styles and health care choices that will preserve and enhance the health status of Federal employees, retirees, and their families.

For the past several years, retirees have been able to make their open season changes on-line through a system provided by OPM. The majority of Federal employees can do so as well through employee express or a comparable system made available to them by their agencies. As part of ongoing automation strategy, and consistent with the president's call for expanding e-government, we piloted several web-based decision-support and information tools on our web site during this year's open season which ended this Monday, December 9th. These tools help individuals rate and rank the health plans available to them based on criteria and preferences they provide.

We will expand the customer-service and satisfaction data and accreditation ratings now available electronically and explore with our health plans ways to enhance their consumer information in conjunction with ours to facilitate putting maximum control over their health and health care in the hands of consumers.

In summary, because we recognize how important the program is to the Government as it seeks to recruit and retain the workforce we need to keep our country safe and secure, we will work even harder to maintain quality and control costs in the FEHB program. We pledge to collaborate with you and with our stakeholders to keep the FEHB program a model for employer provided health care coverage.

I will be happy to answer any questions you may have at this time.

Mr. WELDON. I thank you very much for your testimony.

You were here to listen to the testimony of the first panel, Mr. Hoyer, and he spoke about his legislation to increase the government contribution to FEHBP from 72 percent to 80 percent of the weighted average of premiums and to raise the cap on the share of premiums that the government can pay.

Has OPM estimated the cost of this legislation?

Mr. BLAIR. We have given initial review of what that cost would be, and we've determined it to be $1.7 billion for the first year, 900 of which will be mandatory spending for annuitants.

Mr. WELDON. Thank you very much. That was very helpful.

Mr. BLAIR. We'd be pleased to provide you with the methodology.

Mr. WELDON. Yes. I think I want to have my staff look at that.

As you know, the committee held a hearing this spring to examine cafeteria plans. Witnesses at that hearing told us that cafeteria plans can make it easier for employers to recruit prospective, well-qualified employees and retain good employees, because they allow individual employees to maximize the value of the benefits the employer offers. They are also becoming more prevalent in the private sector.

Cafeteria plans can also be designed to allow employees to use the government's contribution to pay for 100 percent of the health care premiums, if they choose, which is certainly moving above and beyond the direction Mr. Hoyer was speaking about.

Has OPM considered establishing cafeteria plans for Federal employees?

Mr. BLAIR. We have considered it, sir, and we are actually going about doing so in an incremental way. The first step in this was a premium conversion which took place in January 2001. The second step was the implementation of the flexible spending accounts which we will see at the middle of next year.

I believe further legislation, if we want to move in that direction, would be required; and we'd be happy to work with you at reviewing and developing plans.

Mr. WELDON. Can you just give me an idea of what type of enabling legislation you're talking about?

Mr. BLAIR. I think you—it depends on what benefits we're talking about, and there are a whole wide range of benefits that you can have under a cafeteria plan. We want to make sure that the plans are contemporary, that they provide choice for employees. At the same time we would want to contain costs, and we would want to make sure that employees are using their dollars wisely.

I think that we need to develop a set of principles on which to proceed at first. I think that the first two options that I've described regarding premium conversion and FSAs are a good start, but we need—we can and we would like to review different options as well.

Mr. WELDON. Several witnesses at today's hearing will criticize your decision to allow APWU to establish its consumer-driven option. They say it will create adverse selection, which, of course, is one of the issues that is constantly brought up—medical savings accounts as well.

How do you respond to this criticism?

Mr. BLAIR. I think adverse selection is something we should always guard against. The new APWU plan specifically asked for, when she asked for new and innovative plans—there is a trend in the industry now. We certainly don't want to stifle innovation at a time in which we see double-digit increases in our health benefits premiums.

With regards to adverse selection, these are things that we can watch out for in our oversight of the program. We would not have adopted the consumer-driven plan if we thought it would lead to adverse selection. That said, if the trends show over a period of years adverse selection is taking place, we have options available to us to help us contain and restrain that from happening.

Mr. WELDON. Could you share with the committee what some of those options would be?

Mr. BLAIR. Every year we send out a call letter in which we ask the carriers to come back to us with proposals as to what the benefit structure should look like. If we see trends developing in which adverse selection is taking place, this is the time in which we can nip this in the bud, so to speak, in which we can make sure the plans are not going in that direction and make sure that adverse selection is minimized.

Mr. WELDON. Can I get your assurance that you and OPM are willing to work with the committee if issues of adverse selection arise?

Mr. BLAIR. Certainly, sir. Adverse selection is something that we don't want to see arise at all. It impacts negatively on the plan. It increases overall cost at times and is not good for employees. So we will be happy to work with you. We are a stakeholder and we certainly share your concerns about that.

Mr. WELDON. I am pleased to recognize the ranking member for questions.

Mr. DAVIS OF ILLINOIS. Thank you very much, Mr. Chairman.

Mr. Blair, thank you for your testimony and please extend my regards to Director James, if you would.

You indicated in your statement that the Director had initiated the comprehensive outside audit to review mandates of anticipated plans over the past decade so that you can inform Congress about the cost of mandated health care services.

Could you tell us who is conducting the audit and when will it be completed?

Mr. BLAIR. The Hay Group is conducting that audit. We anticipate it to be completed shortly, probably around the first part of the year.

Mr. DAVIS OF ILLINOIS. Do you anticipate that the audit will report health benefits or savings that the plan participants may have derived from these mandated——

Mr. BLAIR. I have not seen a draft report yet, so I really couldn't report on what we anticipate in that.

Mr. DAVIS OF ILLINOIS. Earlier this year OPM announced that the FEHBP premiums would increase 11.1 percent for 2003. You stated that the increase was more than 2 percent better than last year's 13.3 percent increase.

Were any benefits cut to achieve the reduction and, if so, which benefits were they?

Mr. BLAIR. To the best of my knowledge, we had no substantial change in the benefit packages this year, and as a matter of fact, we also urged all of the carriers to also start covering colon cancer screenings as well.

Mr. DAVIS OF ILLINOIS. So you were able to achieve this reduction without reducing benefits?

Mr. BLAIR. We were able to minimize the increase without an across-the-board reduction of benefits.

Mr. DAVIS OF ILLINOIS. Which I think is indeed commendable.

You also stated that the Director's strategy in reducing premiums paid tangible dividend in 2003 by saving taxpayers and plan participants almost $1 billion.

Now, will these savings translate into expanded benefits or better quality health care for plan participants?

Mr. BLAIR. It was a concern that our package was kept level. I think you will see the same level of benefits as you did last year, just a lower rate of increase than what we saw last year.

Mr. DAVIS OF ILLINOIS. So we actually expect that the level of care is going to remain pretty steady, that the individuals will not experience any care reduction or difficulty in accessing benefits?

Mr. BLAIR. There may be some benefit reductions in one of the 188 plans that are offered. That said, there were no benefit reductions across the board. As a matter of fact, we also expanded care in the areas of colon cancer screening, so I think that we got a better bang for our buck this year.

Mr. DAVIS OF ILLINOIS. So individuals, as they choose different plans, they may look at the options that exist there and make determinations, but you are confident that across the board they are actually going to be better off?

Mr. BLAIR. I do not want to say "better off." They should be at the same position that they are today, currently. There may be some cost increases.

I was looking at my plan under Blue Cross/Blue Shield, and the prescription pharmacy benefit, the mail order, did increase in price from, I think, $25 to $35, so that is an instance where you may be paying higher amounts for a 90-day prescription. That said, the benefit that we saw—we said we saw tangible benefits of $1 billion—was in terms of a comparison to the overall average increase nationwide of about 15 percent.

Mr. DAVIS OF ILLINOIS. And you indicated that the new developments in the FEHBP were proposed to contain costs while maintaining quality and choice in the program?

Mr. BLAIR. Yes, sir.

Mr. DAVIS OF ILLINOIS. I understand the notion that consumer-driven plan options contain costs by exposing plan participants to more of the costs of the health benefits and services they use, like prescription drugs, where the costs may go higher than what they were.

How will we be able to guard against the negative effect of adverse selection in consumer-driven plan options?

Mr. BLAIR. What you are going to have to do is see if trends develop over the first few years. This is a new plan being offered by APWU, and we expect to see enrollments of anywhere from 2,000 to 10,000, and that is in a universe of 4 million enrollees. So keep that in mind. We will study that closely because if you start see trends involving adverse risk selection or adverse selection, we can monitor that and help adjust that through our annual call letter proceedings.

No one wants to see adverse selection develop in this, but we are also seeing industry trends in which new plans like the APWU and plans similar to that are being offered to private-sector employees. This may appeal to some. It also appeals to people who because of—who may be shopping because of price, and it does provide a comprehensive benefit at less cost to the enrollee. So this is exactly the kind of innovation we are looking for.

We certainly would not want to stifle it from the beginning; rather, we would want to encourage it. And we want to encourage such kinds of innovation.

That said, part of the role of OPM is to monitor and oversee the program, and we will be very vigilant that the program operates and that it doesn't lead to overall program cost increases for either the Government or enrollees.

Mr. DAVIS OF ILLINOIS. Do you think they will look for a decrease in cost as they develop this plan, if that's what they were trying to do?

Mr. BLAIR. I think they were trying to develop an affordable plan in looking at what the industry trends were, and in looking at that, they saw that this was the kind of plan that had not yet been offered in the FEHBP.

One of the hallmarks of the FEHBP is choice. We want to provide as many choices as possible, and if the industry is developing new and innovative products like this, we certainly should offer it to our enrollees.

Mr. DAVIS OF ILLINOIS. Thank you very much.

Mr. WELDON. I want to thank Mr. Blair, and Mr. Flynn for accompanying him. You didn't have to answer any questions which I guess is good news. We appreciate all of your testimony and we look forward to working with you in the years ahead on these very important issues, and you are dismissed.

Before we bring up the third panel, I have to add some chairs to the table, so we will have a very brief recess here and then we will call those witnesses up.

I apologize to our witnesses for the crowded conditions at the table.

I want to extend a welcome to or third panel. Each of these witnesses has a great deal of experience with the FEHBP and has a great interest in making sure that the program is successful.

Mr. Walt Francis is an economist and the author of the annual Checkbooks Guide to Health Plans for Federal Employees. He is a widely acknowledged expert on FEHBP and has testified before this subcommittee in the past.

Mr. Carroll Midgett is the chief operating manager of the American Postal Workers Union. The APWU's consumer-driven option is one of the most important developments in the FEHBP, and I look forward to hearing more about it.

Ms. Colleen Kelley serves as president of the National Treasury Employees Union. Founded over 55 years ago, NTEU represents some 155,000 workers in 24 government agencies, making it the largest independent nonpostal Federal employees union.

Mr. Charles Fallis serves as president of the National Association of Retired Federal Employees. We welcome you to your first testimony before this subcommittee. Your Congressman, Mr. Davis, did a very nice job, saying kind words about you, and I am looking forward to your testimony as well.

Mr. Bobby Harnage is the president of the American Federation of Government Employees. AFGE is the largest Federal employee union, representing 600,000 Federal and D.C. government workers nationwide and overseas.

Mr. Greg Scandlen is a consultant on health policy and is currently working with the Galen institute of Alexandria, VA. He has written widely on health care issues and is a recognized expert.

As you all know, it is customary for the committee to ask the witnesses to take the oath. Would you all please rise and raise your right hands. I understand we have an expert with APWU, and we will swear you in as well.

[Witnesses sworn.]

Mr. WELDON. Let the court reporter annotate that all witnesses responded in the affirmative.

It is usually customary to proceed beginning at the chairman's left, so we will begin with Mr. Francis, if you would like to give your testimony. I guess you will have to hand the mic around so the court reporter can clearly hear what you are saying. I think you can probably reach that OK.

You may proceed with your testimony. The committee has received your written comments and would ask that you each summarize your verbal testimony in 5 minutes.

You are recognized for 5 minutes, Mr. Francis.

STATEMENTS OF WALTON FRANCIS, ECONOMIST AND AUTHOR; CARROLL E. MIDGETT, CHIEF EXECUTIVE MANAGER, AMERICAN POSTAL WORKER'S UNION; MICHAEL SHOWALTER, VICE PRESIDENT, DEFINITY CARE; COLLEEN M. KELLEY, PRESIDENT, NATIONAL TREASURY UNION; CHARLES L. FALLIS, PRESIDENT, NATIONAL ASSOCIATION OF RETIRED FEDERAL EMPLOYEES; BOBBY L. HARNAGE, SR., PRESIDENT, AMERICAN FEDERATION OF GOVERNMENT EMPLOYEES; AND GREG SCANDLEN, CONSULTANT

Mr. FRANCIS. Thank you very much, Mr. Chairman, members of the subcommittee.

I want to rain a little bit on the parade today. I think the FEHBP is a program in deep trouble. It's got a great market-driven model, but there are too many leaks, too many places where consumer choices aren't playing the role they should, and things are getting worse. I am going to use two major examples to make this point. One of them has to do with retirees on Medicare.

There are about a million and a half of those people. Their situation is roughly as follows: As a practical matter, they are forced to sign up with Medicare Part B upon turning age 65. Next year, that is about a $1,400 premium. If that couple enrolls in Blue Cross Standard Option, which has about a $2,300 premium next year, they are going to pay—in fact, I gave you the wrong number; it is a total of about $4,000 in premiums they will pay next year. That is incredibly expensive, and nobody should have to pay that much for health insurance, but that is what they do, and the overwhelming majority of them sign up for that plan.

What do they get in return? They get unlimited utilization of hospitals, unlimited utilization of doctors, unlimited medical tests all for free. What does that mean in practice? It means they overuse medical care. I have a friend who got four MRI scans last year. He paid zero for those four MRI scans. I don't think he would have had four if he'd had to pay a couple hundred bucks, but what the heck, it was free.

So we have—there is no employee choice here. There is no choice among plans that's worth talking about in this context. There is certainly no consumer driven—you know, do I really need this health care benefit? Is there a cheaper alternative, etc? Just have an inflation.

It is a vast expense, and it is an expense that falls not just on those retirees, it falls on all the employees in the program because they have the same risk pool; it falls on the Medicare program and on the taxpayer.

And why do we have this problem? Because the Medicare statute—and you've got a committee, a sister committee, that's at fault here—the Medicare statute essentially penalizes anyone who postpones buying Part B no matter what their circumstance. You have to make an irrevocable decision as a financial matter at age 65. You've got a 20- or 25-year life span ahead of you; a prudent person will purchase it, and 90-plus percent of them do.

There is no reason at all there has to be this 10 percent of your pay for failing to join Medicare Part B if you are covered by a comprehensive employer-sponsored plan. And it would take the stroke of a pen to change one sentence of the Medicare statute to let people elect to stay, for example, in the Blue Cross plan that they were in before they turned 65. It was good enough for 3 million employees. It was good enough for them in the first 10 years of their retirement. It is only when they turn 65 that they are forced to give up the regular Blue Cross plan, and it is all still in the Standard Option, mind you, but now a different set of benefits kick in. Yeah, they save that $20 a doctor visit and all that, but they are having to pay $1,400 a year for the privilege. And it is in no one's interest to force that on them.

Relatedly, the Medicare statute forbids any health plan from paying any part of the Medicare Part B premium. The Federal Government, or I should say, the OPM, is the only retiree health plan sponsor in America that has this restriction placed on it. There is just no sense to that.

There ought to be options in this program where people can elect not to take Medicare Part B or to take it as a subsidy and be willing to pay something out of pocket to preserve that choice mechanism that several have spoken so eloquently about.

My second example is the savings from prudent plan selection. Blue Cross Standard Option is the predominant plan in this program today. In the D.C. metro area there are six plans that offer significant savings in premium costs over Blue Cross Standard Option. They include GEHA Standard, Mail Handlers Standard—I am forgetting one or two—and several HMO's.

I calculate that if—and I am taking the six-plan average—if an employee elects to join one of those plans instead of Blue Cross Standard, there is about a $1,900 premium saving. On a before-tax basis, $1,000 of that goes to the government and $900 for the employee, which is one way of saying that the government keeps most of the reward for my frugal plan choice.

What's worse, with my premium conversion in place, the reality of it is that the government saves $1,300 if I move to this less expensive plan, and I save only $600. So building in, in recent years, is a systematic reduction in the incentives created for prudent plan selection. These are easy things to fix.

In the case of the employees, there was some talk earlier today of premium reform and increasing the employer's share, an 80 percent payment perhaps, or even paying 100 percent. The right model is a model in which the Federal Government pays 100 percent of the premium up to a given level which might be the 75th percentile of the all plan average, OK—that gets you the same average 75 percent contribution we have now—but it does two important things.

One is it gives employees 100 percent of the savings from choosing a less expensive plan.

No. 2—and I am delighted to see a number of union members in the audience today, because there are 5 percent of the Federal work force who choose not to have any health insurance coverage at all because it is too expensive. I think this is—I won't say the adjective in public. If we were paying 100 percent of the premium for a frugal plan, for a low-cost plan, then those people, many of whom I know and I've counseled, would feel they could afford to buy health insurance, and we would eliminate that terrible gap and that risk exposure.

Let me just conclude if I may—and by the way, that can be done in a budget-neutral way or with some sweetening of the pot. It doesn't really matter; it certainly doesn't have to hurt anyone.

There are many other reforms needed. We need more plans to offer. There is adverse selection in this plan. It is significant. The reason Blue Cross High Option went out of the program was adverse selection. I think it is a systematic problem, and it can be reduced.

Final point, many conservatives, Heritage Foundation and others, have extolled the virtues of this program as a model for the Nation; a few liberals have. Bill Bradley, 2 years ago, offered a solution based on a FEHBP-type model. I was pleased as punch last Sunday to hear Al Gore on national television saying he was going to develop a health care plan based on the FEHBP model.

I think there is a wide agreement that there is a valuable model here across the political spectrum. What is incumbent on this Congress and on this committee and on the Ways and Means Committee in particular is to take those reform steps that will improve the function in this program for all concerned. We all gain when employees make frugal choices. It reduces the premium for everyone, and to the taxpayer, and there is no reason not to make those improvements.

Thank you.

Mr. WELDON. Thank you, Mr. Francis.

[The prepared statement of Mr. Francis follows:]

TESTIMONY OF WALTON FRANCIS

AUTHOR AND INDEPENDENT CONSULTANT

BEFORE THE SUBCOMMITTEE ON THE CIVIL SERVICE, CENSUS AND AGENCY REORGANIZATION

COMMITTEE ON GOVERNMENT REFORM

U.S. HOUSE OF REPRESENTATIVES

DECEMBER 11, 2002

Mr. Chairman, and members of the Subcommittee:

I am pleased to testify before you today concerning the current status and performance of the Federal Employees Health Benefits Program (FEHBP). As you know, total spending in this program in 2003 will be approximately $27 billion for premiums, and several billion dollars more in enrollee cost sharing. Nine million people depend on it for health care. It is a large responsibility for the Office of Personnel Management and for the Congress.

The program is a remarkable success among Federal health insurance programs, both for its ability to control costs and for its ability to meet enrollee needs. As I discuss later, it is perennially cited as a model for national health insurance reforms. I won't dwell on its successes because these have been amply explained in many previous writings (see Francis 1993a, Francis 1999, and Moffit 2001 for evaluations).

Meeting enrollee health care needs through choice among plans is perhaps the program's strongest feature. Just last week, I counseled a mother who needed a better therapy benefit for her autistic child. The plan she was in paid for 25 visits to an occupational therapist; I identified one for her that paid for 60 visits. A few years ago, a friend who works for a Fortune 500 company mentioned that she was very unhappy with her company's health benefits plan because it didn't pay for acupuncture. This limitation was imposed by headquarters bureaucrats and their health care consulting firm. She was incredulous when I told her that Federal employees in the DC area had a dozen or so plans offering this benefit. And she couldn't believe that this had been decided not by some faceless bureaucrat in the Office of Personnel Management, but by the decisions of employees and plans in deciding what benefit variations were mutually advantageous. In the FEHBP, most decisions are made by enrollees who vote with their feet, not by fiat.

I am particularly pleased with the spirit of reform that OPM Director James is bringing to this program, and with the early fruits of that spirit: a new APWU Consumer-driven plan that is an exciting addition to the array of enrollee choices, and a renewed emphasis on cost control. The FEHBP continues to outperform the private sector in cost containment, and would certainly outperform Medicare if that program did not use the government's ability to put health care providers out of business to impose draconian and arbitrary controls on provider payments. Of course, it far outperforms both in meeting enrollee coverage preferences.

However, the program is in trouble and will gradually lose its effectiveness if significant reforms are not made. I am here today to talk about these problems, and solutions to them.

I testify today in my capacities as an economist expert in program evaluation and policy analysis, and expert on health insurance, not in my capacity as provider of consumer information and advice on health insurance choices. In the interest of disclosure, I want to inform you that although I have testified before Congress a number of times on this program, and had always earned royalties through book sales to Federal agencies, this year there is a change. I will earn royalties from an OPM decision to purchase access to *CHECKBOOK's 2003 Guide to Health Plans for Federal Employees* for 1.8 million annuitants. The details of such purchasing decisions are not within my control or decision, and OPM plays a far smaller role in my life than it does in the lives of the unions and plan executives who testify before you. I will in fact be critical of OPM today. Although I am a great fan of OPM for its ongoing program management skills, OPM has never devoted the resources to analyze in depth, or forcefully argued, for legislative reforms that are vital to the long run success of this program.

Summary. In summary, I believe that the program continues to perform reasonably well, a result of its basic design as a competitive system that is largely driven by market forces. In essence, plans compete for customers through their performance in controlling costs, providing good benefits, and providing good service. Plans that best meet employee and retiree preferences over time gain market share. OPM serves as a neutral facilitator. Both government and enrollees benefit from holding down premium costs over time. The program has become a model. I once wrote an article about the program that the American Enterprise Institute chose to title "A Health Care Program Run by the Federal Government That Works" (Francis 1993b).

Despite the seemingly huge premium increases of recent years, the program continues to outperform the private sector. The enrollment-weighted average premium for 2002 rose 13.1 percent over 2001 (less than stated in the fall 2001 press release because of Open Season plan switching.) The just-released Mercer survey of employer insurance costs found that private sector plans' 2002 premiums rose an average of 15 percent (Martinez 2002). And this FEHBP cost advantage arose despite the continue aging of the Federal work force.

However, the program is showing its age. It has a number of important defects, most of which would require Congressional action to repair. Furthermore, recent and impending reforms to enable employees to use after tax dollars to purchase health care attenuate the ability of the program to contain costs. However desirable these reforms may be as a matter of compensation reform, their undesirable side effect is to diminish the power of market forces in imposing discipline upon spending by health plans and by enrollees. The reforms I advocate include:

- Adding mechanisms to control risk selection in the FEHBP
- Premium redesign to reward frugal enrollees
- Improving the coordination of Medicare and the FEHBP
- Eliminating arbitrary constraints on plan reimbursement for retirees on Medicare
- Admitting new plans to the program
- Reducing mandates in the FEHBP
- Expanding the program to cover military workers dependents
- Marketing the FEHBP system to private and public employers and associations

Time does not permit in depth analysis of each of these issues and options today, but I would be glad to work with the Committee in addressing any of these in more detail. The Committee could easily enlist the Congressional Budget Office, the OPM actuaries, or the Office of Management and Budget, to assist it in exploring these and related options. I strongly recommend that it do so.

How the FEHBP Saves Money. The workings of the market and the forces of competition are abstract concepts. It is useful in assessing performance to address real world effects. I would like to focus on two of these--prescription drug costs and premium savings, and then discuss potential affects on these for the reforms I recommend that the Congress make in this program.

First, consider drugs. For the last decade FEHBP plans have been struggling with increases in prescription drug costs. These increases have resulted primarily from the introduction of new brand name drugs that provide increased protection against disability and disease. As a dramatic example, about two weeks ago the Food and Drug Administration approved a new drug called Forteo that will treat osteoporosis by **restoring** bone density. This is a dramatic advance in treatment for this crippling and life destroying disease. It will reduce expensive surgery and hospitalization for hip fractures in older women. The wholesale price of this drug will be approximately $20 per day, over $7000 a year. And treatment with this drug will require up to two years, for a total cost approaching $14,000 per patient.

Facing increased costs that are very substantial, though on average not nearly this dramatic, FEHBP plans have progressively instituted cost saving measures through benefit redesign. As an example, consider the largest plan, Blue Cross Standard Option. In 1994 this plan charged enrollees 20 percent of the price of prescription drugs, after a $50 deductible. Medicare-participating enrollees paid **nothing** for drugs. Drugs could only be bought through retail pharmacies. Ten years later, for 2003, Blue Cross requires enrollees to pay 25 percent, but only $10 per generic drug and $35 per brand-name drug for a 90 day mail order supply, with no deductible. However, Medicare-participating enrollees now pay **the same** as younger enrollees. During the same 10 year period, most other national plans made similar adjustments, raising cost sharing disproportionately for the heaviest users of drugs, those over age 65. During this period most HMOs raised cost sharing dramatically for the most expensive name brand drugs. Most HMOs now use a six tier price structure, with the highest prices for what are called "non-formulary" name brand drugs.

What has been the result of all these increases in cost sharing? We learn part of the answer from a recent article by RAND scientists (Joyce 2002). Steps such as these substantially reduce spending on drugs, by a fourth or more for the kinds of changes made by most FEHBP plans over the last decade. For example, going from a 1-tier copayment of $10, a design common ten years ago, to a 3-tier copayment of $10/$20/$30 for generic, preferred name-brand, and non-preferred name-brand, reduces current drug spending by about $125 annually among employees. Most of this saving shows up in lower premium costs, mostly recouped by employers who generally save 75 percent or more. To put these numbers in perspective, a saving of $125 per enrollee (and savings in the FEHBP have probably been far more, since the Blue Cross reduction for Medicare participating enrollees was far larger than what RAND analyzed) represents about $500 million annually. This is composed of a saving to enrollees of about $125 million in premiums (largely offset by increased copayments) and a saving to the Federal Treasury of about $375 million annually (and probably much more). This major saving took place without any conscious decision making by Federal bureaucrats or legislative enactments, simply through the workings of a competitive market for health insurance responsive to enrollee decisions.

Second, consider low premium plans. In 2003, the average FEHBP premium is about $8,900 for families. OPM and individual Federal departments and agencies pay about three fourths of this cost for annuitants and employees, respectively. However, what they pay is not a fixed amount. It depends on the plan chosen. Without going into the complex computational details, here are some illustrative savings from the Washington DC metropolitan area, using the government share for GS employees and annuitants.

As shown in the table that follows, there are six plans available in the DC area with premiums that reduce the government share. The three national plans, and many comparable HMO plans, are available around the nation. On average and in round numbers, a family that switches into one of these plans from Blue Cross Standard option will save the Federal government about $1,000 and save the family about $900 (using nominal premium dollars before tax savings). If as few as one percent of all families made this change in Open Season, total savings would be about $300 million to the government and almost as much to enrollees.

Plan	Total 2003 Family Premium	Government Share 2003	Employee Share 2003	Government Savings with Switch from Blue Cross Standard	Employee Savings with Switch from Blue Cross Standard
Blue Cross Standard	$9,226	$6,490	$2,736	NA	NA
Blue Cross Basic	$8,557	$6,418	$2,139	$73	$597
GEHA Standard	$6,500	$4,875	$1,625	$1,615	$1,111
Mail Handlers Standard	$6,341	$4,756	$1,585	$1,734	$1,151
Kaiser Mid-Atlantic	$7,626	$5,719	$1,906	$771	$829
Aetna High	$8,282	$6,212	$2,071	$278	$665
Aetna Standard	$6,434	$4,826	$1,608	$1,665	$1,127
6 Plan Ave. Before Tax	$7,290	$5,467	$1,822	$1,023	$913
6 Plan Ave. After Tax	$7,290	$6,074	$1,216	$1,327	$609

These are not fantasy numbers. My rough estimates show that had all enrollees in 2002 stayed in the same plans as in 2001, the total premium cost would have been $24.6 billion. But through migration to lower cost plans during Open Season, total premium spending was about $24.2 billion, some $400 million lower. (OPM actuaries can provide a more precise estimate.)

The point of these calculations, for both prescription drugs and Open Season migration, is to demonstrate that substantial sums of money are involved in the dynamics of this program. Reforms that improve its performance can result in large savings to both government and enrollees; reforms that reduce its performance can cost far more than their nominal cost.

It is against this backdrop that I assess recent and pending program changes, and a number of reforms that would improve the program.

Tax Preferred Health Care Spending. One of the least understood features of the U.S. Tax Code is that it hugely advantages health care spending by upper bracket taxpayers compared to lower income Americans. With both the so-called "employer share" and "employee share" of health insurance premiums sheltered from taxes, and with Flexible Spending Accounts, the typical Fortune 500 professional employee's family will reap a tax saving of close to $4,000 from total health care spending (premium and out-of-pocket) of $10,000. There is certainly a powerful argument that Federal government employees should be treated equivalently, and that Federal employee compensation should be reformed over time to more closely emulate business practice. I commend OPM for emphasis on reforming compensation policy.

There are, however, costs of this approach. First and most obvious, while a Fortune 500 company gains this huge cost saving for its employees at the expense of the taxpayer at large, the Federal government has no such luxury. "Premium Conversion" and other tax sheltered health care spending directly cost the government in revenues what the employees gain, on a dollar for dollar basis.

Unfortunately, they cost even more. Second, there is an additional cost because some employees have a choice between Federal insurance and their spouse's private insurance. About 5 percent of Federal employees have previously elected to rely on private rather than Federal insurance. Premium Conversion, by improving the relative attractiveness of the FEHBP, has undoubtedly cause many of these to switch. I have seen no data, but if even 1 percent of employees (one out of five of those previously enrolled in private plans) have switched to the FEHBP, the cost to the government is in the ballpark of $200 million a year. (I would suggest to the Committee that it ask the OPM actuaries for an analysis of this cost.)

Third, and far worse from the perspective of the FEHBP as a dynamic program, the savings from switching to lower premium plans have been reduced. The figures above on potential savings of roughly $1,000 a year to the government and $900 to enrollees from such Open Season choices are based on before tax dollars. After tax, the benefits to employees of switching are reduced by approximately one third, in this case to $600, while government savings reach $1300 (see Francis, 2002). This is a substantial attenuation of incentives to enrollees who are, after all, the ones who make the decisions. Moreover, the reason premiums are lower in some of these plans is that benefits are more frugal. It is possible with under Premium Conversion some employees will migrate the other way, costing rather than saving the government on average about $1300 per switch. In other words, the government has in the name of compensation policy substantially reduced the immediate cost saving incentives in the program.

As a further result, plans will over time undoubtedly choose to increase both benefits and premiums rather than exercise frugality, since there is a one-third subsidy to increased generosity or, conversely, a one-third penalty for frugality. Interestingly, the impending addition of Flexible Spending Accounts will make the incentive structure worse for out of pocket costs as well, but will at least offset somewhat the bias towards expanding premiums and reducing copayments.

Proposed legislation that would extend to retirees the same tax preference realized by employees will further decrease what few incentives exist today for frugal decisions by plans and enrollees for the retired population. (I note that no private retirees have such a tax preference, and that Medicare premiums paid by the aged are not tax preferred.)

None of these criticisms should be taken to mean that Federal employees should not be put on an equal footing with the private sector in terms of compensation policy. However, they do mean that reform of the antiquated FEHBP incentive structure is all the more urgent and vital to the future performance of the program. I urge the Committee to favorably consider such reforms. In a different context, adding a prescription drug benefit is the potential carrot for Medicare reform. I think that tax preferences should be the carrot for FEHBP reform.

Controlling Risk Selection in the FEHBP. The FEHBP is remarkably stable. Although enrollees vote with their feet in Open Season, most of those who should change plans do not. This is despite my utmost efforts, through my annual *Guide* and through television, radio, and speaking engagements, to persuade enrollees to save themselves a lot of money by switching to better plans. For 1992 the *Guide* estimated that an annuitant couple without Medicare would pay more than double in premiums and out of pocket costs to enroll in Blue Cross High option rather than Blue Cross Standard option, an excess cost of about $3200. For 2001, ten years later and the final year of the Blue Cross High option plan, we estimated a yearly saving of $700 (the premium differential had steadily shrunk over the years.) Yet, despite these immense savings, some combination of brand loyalty, fear, ignorance, and (for a few) slightly better benefits kept a large number of mostly aged enrollees in the High option. In that ten year period High option enrollment only declined from 125,000 to 98,000.

This inertia will equally well serve to reduce any adverse selection effects from the new APWU Consumer-driven plan. I doubt that this plan will draw mainly from low cost enrollees. But even if it did so, and gained hundreds of thousands of enrollees over a several year period, the effect on the program as a whole would be imperceptible.

Age Category	Family Size	Average Health Care Spending
Under 35	1	$1,100
35-44	1	$2,200
45-54	1	$2,500
55-64	1	$4,600
65-74	1	$4,600
75+	1	$6,500
Under 35	2	$1,800
35-44	2	$3,900
45-54	2	$4,200
55-64	2	$7,100
65-74	2	$7,500
75+	2	$13,500

Ironically, however, the Blue Cross High option should be alive and well today. It was a good plan that suffered an unfair fate. Despite the fact that it attracted a greatly disproportionate share of elderly enrollees, and especially the elderly without Medicare, it received the same government contribution as the plans with an average mix of high cost enrollees. To understand the importance of risk selection, consider 1997 data from the Medical Expenditure Panel Survey, which is the most authoritative source of detailed information on health care spending by age.

As these data show, average health care spending increases astronomically with age. A new Federal hire just out of college has an expected spending of less than one fifth of an older retiree. Blue Cross High option was unreasonably expensive not because of some flaw in benefit design or administration, but simply because it attracted a disproportionate number of 65 and 75 year old annuitants: older, sicker, and far more expensive. (For an extended discussion of risk selection issues, see the 1989 CRS study that remains timely today.)

Under current law, the FEHBP program averages these risks and charges individual enrollees the same amount regardless of age, distinguishing only between self only and families of two or more. This seems to be a perfectly reasonable approach to "fairness" in compensation policy, though the resulting high premium charge for younger workers is one of the main reasons why 5 percent or more of the Federal work force, mostly younger workers, has no health insurance at all. But it is a flawed approach to premium design in a market driven system. Furthermore, in practice it fails to achieve its equity objective because the plans that disproportionately attract older enrollees have to charge a higher premium to break even, and the older and sicker wind up paying more.

Instead, the statute should be amended to allow the government to pay differential amounts to plans based on the age and Medicare status of enrollees. The share that enrollees pay in any given risk category could be "held harmless" on average. There is absolutely no reason why 75 year olds without Medicare should be penalized by having to pay double or triple the premiums of younger enrollees for selecting plans, like Blue Cross High option, that are just slightly more annuitant friendly than plans that cater to younger enrollees.

Put another way, the current statute says, in effect, that the government should pay 75 percent of the premium for all enrollees, taken as an average. But it could say, instead, that the government will pay 90 percent for those over age 75 without Medicare, 50 percent of a much lower premium for those under age 55, and still pay 75 percent on average. Amended to adjust for age-related risk it would allow enrollees to select the best plans without having to flee those plans that attract a disproportionate number of union shop stewards (older and more expensive), diabetics, annuitants age 55 to 64, and 75 year old annuitants without Medicare.

One very important risk factor, in this context, is Medicare status. With Medicare as the primary payer for the great majority of annuitants over age 65, FEHBP plans only have to pay residual expenses. These can be very high, but it appears that plans prosper by attracting this group. A majority of enrollees in Blue Cross Standard option, for example, are annuitants with Medicare.

Devising a risk adjusted premium that will be fair to all groups, both in reality and as perceived by advocates, will potentially be politically and actuarially complex. But it can be done, without descending into the swamp of details that has made risk adjustment in Medicare a political and programmatic disaster. Adjusting for nothing more than two age categories (above and below 55) and Medicare status will greatly attenuate the bizarre incentives to both plans and enrollees created by current premium sharing arrangements. The Congress need not (and in my view should not) attempt to write a rigid formula. For those with a long memory, the original design of the FEHBP called for a 60 percent government share of premium, but due to drafting myopia and a bizarre "big six" formula wound up with a 73 percent share of premium. Instead, the Congress could simply mandate that OPM devise an actuarially fair system that will not penalize any group by more than a few percent in the amount of premium it pays.

There are alternative ways to reduce risk selection in the program. For example, the risks from enrollees with costs above (for example) $100,000 in a year could be pooled and reinsured, so that the smaller plans and those with disproportionate shares of older and more expensive enrollees did not face a disproportionate cost burden. I have heard that one of the better small plans left the program a decade ago because of a multi-million dollar premature birth disaster.

If the enrollee share of premium for each plan bore a reasonably rational relationship to plan benefits, without the artificial effects of adverse risk selection by age and Medicare status, then plans could concentrate their energies on devising benefit and service reforms that best served their customers. In this regard, while the plans have often been accused of using benefit design decisions to "cherry pick" to get the healthiest enrollees, it is apparent that such behavior has been infrequent. Indeed, some of the plans with the strongest incentives to do so have not only not skewed benefits, but also gone out of business through "failing" to do so. This, of course, is due in part to OPM's stewardship in reviewing plan change proposals. Regardless, any reform that reduces risk selection or its costs also reduces incentives to plans to design benefits to discriminate against sicker enrollees.

As a matter of equity, such a reform would also reduce the unfair penalty that the current program imposes on those who, through no fault of their own, face far higher health care costs than average. To enroll in plans with the best coverages, these elderly and chronically ill patients have to pay a premium differential that is even higher than the actuarial value of those benefits.

Premium Redesign. Under current law the government nominally gets 75 percent (or more, for postal and FDIC employees) of the premium saving from frugal plan choices made by enrollees. The higher the government share, the less incentive enrollees have to choose frugal plan designs. Paradoxically, the seemingly enrollee friendly "Premium Conversion" reform reduced the incentive to shop frugally by reducing the *de facto* employee share of employee premiums from 25 percent to about 17 percent (varying with the precise tax bracket of each employee). And plans now have correspondingly reduced incentives to keep premiums down.

There is one key feature in existing premium design that prevents an early disaster. With the government contribution pegged to the average plan cost, and the government paying no more than 75 percent of that level, enrollees pay the entire excess cost of plans that cost more than average. High cost plans are not rewarded in the FEHBP. But frugal plans and frugal purchasing decisions have never been well rewarded, and are now poorly rewarded. Alain Enthoven recently argued pungently that current employer health insurance contributions generally reward the health care equivalent of gas-guzzlers that are both expensive and unreliable, but should instead reward "Honda" health plans (Enthoven 2002). In his words, what we "need is for most employers to offer multiple choice and expose employees to **full** responsibility for premium differences" (emphasis added).

It is possible to adjust the government contribution formula to improve the incentives for "Hondas." For example, if the government share were made 100 percent of premium up to 70 percent of the all plan average, and nothing thereafter, the overall contribution would still be near 75 percent of the all plan average. However, incentives would change radically. Employees would now keep all of the savings from selection of lower cost plans. Enrollment in the six plans listed above would jump. But the most important effect would occur over time: plans would selectively reduce the generosity of benefits to keep premiums down, and employees who became more frugal users of health care as copayments increased would help drive down the overall costs and premiums of the entire program.

Less drastic formula changes could achieve any desired mix of incentives and rewards. For example, a formula paying 90 percent of premium up to 80 percent of the all plan average would also result in an overall government subsidy of about 75 percent, but focus incentives for both plans and enrollees on less drastic changes in plan design.

Under either of these options, plans would have greatly increased incentives to devise cost sharing provisions that, like their prescription drug benefits, would reduce overall utilization costs and hence unnecessarily large premiums.

Note also that under either formula suggested above, the enrollee premium share for a frugal plan would be reduced, and the incentive of healthy, young employees to enroll in the FEHBP significantly increased. These enrollees would, on average, reduce overall premium costs and help to reduce the premium creep created by a rapidly aging Federal work force. In other words, these are employee-friendly reform ideas, to be welcomed rather than feared.

Finally, premium reform along the lines above is not only compatible with, but also mutually supportive of, creation of tax-advantaged Flexible Spending Accounts. Those Accounts would reduce the sting of any increased copayments, while further rewarding frugality in spending the employees' own money.

Medicare and FEHBP Coordination. Medicare and the FEHBP were each created about 40 years ago, and the design of each has not significantly changed since its inception. Medicare remains frozen in the time warp of vintage 1960 insurance patterns (e.g., the nonsensical bifurcation between hospital and physician costs, and the failure to cover prescription drugs). The FEHBP has aged far more gracefully, with a market driven structure that readily adopts the latest and best insurance practices. But neither program has made any sensible accommodation to the existence of the other.

Almost all retirees elect to pay the Medicare Part B premium at age 65, and then enroll in one of the national fee for service plans. This pattern overwhelmingly dominates retiree choices because these plans offer wraparound coverage that in almost all cases allows enrollees to go to any providers (whether or not preferred) and pay nothing at all for hospital or physician services if they enroll in Part B. HMOs could offer comparable incentives, but only a few do so because they would have no comparative advantage. This wonderful coverage comes, however, at a high price. In 2003, enrollees who pay both FEHBP and Medicare will in some cases double their premium cost. For example, one of the better choices for single enrollees for 2003 is GEHA Standard option, a choice that cost $720 a year without Part B and $1,420 a year with Part B. A couple enrolled in the most popular retiree plan, Blue Cross Standard option, will pay Blue Cross $2,700 and Medicare another $1,400, for a total premium cost of over $4,000.

This same couple was most likely enrolled in Blue Cross while employed, and until age 65, and was satisfied with its good benefits and reasonable premium. What changed upon turning age 65 that impelled them to pay an extra $1,400 a year to get roughly half as much back from reduced cost sharing? (The *Guide* estimates that the net effect of joining Part B is to cost the average retired couple in Blue Cross Standard option an extra $500 a year.) The answer is that this decision is rational for that couple only because existing law is irrational.

Of greater importance to the program and to the United States Treasury, this decision is expensive. That retired couple has no incentive to be frugal in any way in making decisions about any kind of health care other than prescription drugs and dental care. Unlimited provider visits are free. The most expensive provider in the state or city is free. The most discretionary surgical procedure is free. Durable medical equipment is free. Every conceivable medical test is free. Thousand dollar MRI and CAT scans are free. Based on the general findings of the effects of cost sharing from health care utilization research, that couple costs the Federal government somewhere on the order of $2,000 in unnecessary medical care utilization. With approximately 1.5 million Medicare enrollees (both single and couples), the Federal government loses on the order of $2 billion a year under the current system. Most of this cost falls on Medicare (which pays first) but many hundreds of millions fall on the FEHBP.

Under existing law, that couple cannot postpone indefinitely the decision to enroll in Part B. After age 65, there is a 10 percent a year penalty for every year the decision is delayed. (Presumably the reason for the penalty was to prevent risk selection. But that rationale makes no sense when the retiree is enrolled in an insurance plan as good or better than Medicare.) Within a few years, the original decision not to enroll becomes financially irreversible. No matter how comfortable that couple is with Blue Cross alone before age 65, failure to enroll in Part B exposes them for the rest of their lives to the vicissitudes of the political process, and to unknown hazards from insurance gaps. A recent Nobel prize went to economists who have studied issues like these and found that ordinary humans are risk averse and will make an actuarially adverse decision to avoid any possibility of future loss. The Federal government imposes a cruel tax on retirees with the Part B penalty. The Federal government also imposes a stupid tax on itself with that penalty. State and local governments and Fortune 500 companies shed themselves of retiree health care obligations at age 65 simply because virtually without exception retirees pay to join Part B at age 65 rather than postpone that decision and remain in the employer sponsored plan.

Alternatively, the Congress could enact legislation to allow retirees to join Part B at any age without penalty, provided that until the time of enrollment they were covered by an employer-sponsored health plan. With such a change, Medicare program costs would be greatly reduced (how much depending on subsequent employer decisions--many today pay retirees' Part B premium to induce them to join Medicare). FEHBP costs would rise, but the net effect to the Federal Treasury would be significantly positive. Incidentally, this same penalty-free postponement option is available to public and private employees who work past age 65, so this reform would hardly violate some time-hallowed rigid line demarcating that age.

There is an equally useful reform available to the Congress that would save FEHBP more than Medicare, but also benefit the Treasury overall. In the late 1990's, for reasons never documented publicly, the bureaucrats who run Medicare and the Congressional staff on the Ways and Means and Finance committees quietly inserted a special penalty on the FEHBP into the Medicare statute. No FEHBP plan is allowed to subsidize the purchase of Part B. The Federal government is now the only employer in America that cannot defray the cost of Medicare for its retirees. This perplexing enactment verged likely costs Medicare more than it saves. It certainly costs the Treasury far more than it saves. Were FEHBP plans still allowed to pay Part B premiums, they would likely begun to do so over time, paying partial premiums rather than eliminating copayments within their available budget flexibility. Certainly this would have been a hugely attractive option to HMOs. And despite the hard times that have fallen upon HMOs in recent years, they still save money compared to fee for service. With an average total cost (both premium and out of pocket) $800 lower than national plans, shifting as few as ten percent of retirees with Medicare from fee for service to HMOs would save almost $100 million a year.

These two reforms--allowing plans to pay Part B premiums and allowing enrollees to postpone or suspend Medicare Part B without penalty while enrolled in an employer sponsored plan--have the potential to save both retirees and the government hundreds of millions of dollars annually.

Eliminating Arbitrary Constraints on Medicare Enrollees. In the late 1990's OPM imposed two completely unnecessary and harmful constraints on Medicare-participating enrollees (it is possible that these constraints are dictated by law; but if that is so the Congress should change the law). First, OPM appears to have required plans to eliminate coverages available to employees if Medicare does not cover those benefits. To take a dramatic example, over ninety percent of all health plans cover pancreas transplants. This is a mainstream medical procedure. However, the Medicare bureaucracy has not yet decided to cover this procedure except as part of a combined kidney-pancreas transplant. An enrollee in Blue Cross who needs the life saving pancreas-only procedure at age 64 can get it. After age 65, simply by having enrolled in Part B, this enrollee will be denied the procedure and probably die a lingering death. There is no excuse of any kind for this kind of restriction. Medicare is notoriously slow in approving new Medical procedures and devices. Why should Federal retirees be forced to give up benefits--and there are hundreds of accepted procedures that Medicare denies--simply because another Federal agency denies them to its customers? FEHBP plans should be required, in coordinating benefits with Medicare, to pay for any procedure allowed **either** by Medicare or the plan itself for under age 65 enrollees. The FEHBP should not be a party to arbitrary "gotchas" denying useful benefits.

Second, OPM appears to have imposed by administrative fiat a peculiar restriction on provider participation for those participating in Medicare. For reasons rooted in Medicare's bureaucratic history, absurdity, and partisan politics, Medicare law effectively prohibits what is called "private contracting" (see Hoff 1998). Doctors can be jailed for Medicare fraud if they accept patients willing to pay more than the Medicare payment rules, even if both the patient and the physician agree to deal outside the Medicare system. At age 64, a retiree enrolled in Blue Cross can use any physician of his or her choice, accepting the payment penalty if the physician charges more than Blue Cross accepts as a reasonable fee, but nonetheless getting roughly half the bill reimbursed. At age 65, that same retiree, newly enrolled in Medicare, is denied by OPM the ability to obtain any reimbursement for that same physician service if the physician refuses to participate in Medicare or insists on a surcharge for his or her particularly skilled treatments.

To the best of my knowledge, these arbitrary and unreasonable restrictions could be eliminated by a stroke of the OPM Director's pen. At worst, they could be eliminated by the Congress in a one sentence legislative change to the Title 5 of the U.S. Code.

Admitting New Plans to the Program. When the FEHBP statute was enacted, the political imperative that led to its marvelous design was the preservation of existing union and employee organization plans under the political principal of "grandfathering the status quo". This political imperatives led to the creation of virtually the only Federal program driven by consumer decisions. The statute, as enacted, allowed unlimited free entry to "comprehensive" plans, interpreted by OPM to mean only HMOs, but no free entry to fee for service plans. A brief open window on new union plans in the early 1980's led to a half dozen new entrants from unions such as AFGE, NTEU, and others, that later folded. A few national plans, notably Blue Cross, GEHA, and APWU have creatively introduced new options in the last several years. However, as things stand now, if a responsible insurance company wanted to participate in the FEHBP with an innovative new fee for service plan that would save the program money, it would take an act of Congress to admit it. (Actually, there is an interesting argument that the OPM Director could expansively interpret "comprehensive" to admit additional plans under existing law.)

This restriction serves no useful purpose. Any plan that can demonstrate fiscal solvency and meet the other oversight standards that OPM quite reasonably imposes on participating plans should be available to Federal employees and annuitants. There is a spurious argument that the total number of available plans should be held to some limited number, on the grounds that employees have a limited capacity to review and interpret plans. But the fact is that from day one of this program, 40 years ago, the number of available plans exceeded the ability of ordinary humans to review and evaluate. No one is forced to read 10 or 20 or 30 or 40 plan brochures just because that number of plans is available in an area. Furthermore, friends and neighbors, OPM itself, newspapers and magazines, CHECKBOOK's *Guide*, and even our competitor PlanSmartChoice all provide helpful information to assist in comparing plans (of course, I do not view all these sources as **equally** helpful.) Consumers deal quite handily with the availability of hundreds of automobile choices, each differing in important and complex ways which are only comprehensible to engineers. Adding a few dozen or even a few hundred health plans to the FEHBP creates no important problems. In fact, five years ago there were approximately 200 more plans participating in the program than there are today, a major reduction in plan choice caused primarily by consolidation and retrenchment among HMOs.

Some of the existing union participants, such as NALC and PBP, may well decide to emulate GEHA, Blue Cross, and APWU with new plan options. I hope they will do so, and urge them to do so. But the program's future should not depend on the decisions of unions whose primary purpose, after all is said and done, is not to administer health insurance.

The Congress should amend the statute to allow either unlimited entry into the program or, if there are administrative concerns, entry of a "reasonable" number of plans each year as determined by OPM. There is no reason to limit such offerings to plans sponsored by unions, a restriction that does not apply to HMOs in any event. I understand that OPM is proposing legislation that would achieve this purpose and recommend enactment if it does not newly empower OPM to dictate the details of plan offerings. (This would be an unnecessary power of discretion that the Congress should resist strongly, since it directly contradicts the principle of consumer sovereignty in this program and because the OPM track record on mandated benefits demonstrates the danger of giving OPM regulatory authority over detailed benefit design.)

Reducing mandates in the FEHBP. During the 1990s, OPM added a substantial number of mandated coverages to the FEHBP, mostly at White House instigation. One ineffectual mandate was enacted by the Congress for reasons of sloganeering. The most well known mandate was mental health parity. I think that the parity requirement was a good one, despite its potential expense. Many of the others were of dubious utility and some have even been shown to be medically worthless. More importantly than any it added were the ones that OPM did not remove: state-mandated benefits.

Director James recently took the important step of exempting FEHBP plans from expensive accounting standards developed for procurement of complex weapons systems and inappropriate to health insurance, despite the (fallacious) assertion that these standards were needed to prevent fraud. This is the kind of decision making that the FEHBP needs.

I understand that OPM is studying the costs of both Federal and state mandates. Depending on the precise results of this study, OPM should eliminate as many mandates as can reasonably be justified. In this respect, the standard for retention should not be that the benefit is desired by many enrollees, or is useful to the health of many enrollees. OPM should retain a medical mandate only if it can be shown by strong scientific evidence to be essential to health for many enrollees **and** shown that few if any plans would offer the benefit absent the mandate. I think that mental health parity, particularly for hospitalization, meets this test. Very few other mandates do. For example, female enrollees can be trusted to select plans with reasonable mammography benefits; appropriately evolving over time with increasing scientific evidence. OPM need not and should not intrude in this complex and controversial issue by establishing a schedule of required mammography benefits. Similarly, OPM should not attempt to dictate childhood immunization schedules, prostate exams, treatment options for breast cancer, or a host of other benefit details that far exceed both its competence and its ability to correct errors.

Expanding the Program to Cover Military Personnel. The FEHBP does not cover almost half of all Federal employees and dependents: U.S. Military personnel and their dependents. This is particularly anomalous because the medical skills and equipment needed for military preparedness and operations, such as emergency medicine and surgery, are not those associated with pediatric, obstetrical, and other civilian-oriented services that comprise the overwhelming majority of DOD sponsored health care. While the tens of thousands of high ranking officers who constitute the military health establishment are unlikely to voluntarily relinquish their bureaucratic turf and give up their well paid administrative jobs, the Secretary of Defense has voiced concern over the huge resources devoted to DOD sponsored health care. The Tricare system is unpopular with military dependents. There is no reason that the FEHBP statute should not be amended to provide OPM authority to fold any or all military families into the FEHBP for non-service related health care, upon reasonable premium contributions by the Department of Defense. Providing legal discretion to OPM to implement this option in the future need not await, or depend upon, the views of the uniformed service brass.

If such a reform ever came to pass, the DOD might well decide to fund a higher percentage of premium cost than received by most civilian employees, because military personnel pay no or very low premiums. This would not depart significantly from the current FEHBP model, which allows for higher government premium shares in the Postal Service and FDIC. A proper study of military health care costs (many of which are concealed within base budgets for facilities and equipment) would undoubtedly show that DOD could save a great deal of money by dismantling Tricare and buying into the FEHBP, even if it had to pay full premiums.

Marketing the FEHBP System to Private and Public Employers and Associations. There have been recurring calls over the years to export the FEHBP model to the private sector, and extolling it even as a model for Medicare reform. Analysts at think tanks like the Heritage Foundation and American Enterprise Institute have long suggested this idea. Most recently, respected health care analysts Stan Dorn and Jack Meyer have suggested a strategy by which the FEHBP model could be replicated in the Labor Department and used in conjunction with tax credits to provide insurance to the unemployed (Dorn 2002). Just last Sunday former Vice President Al Gore stated on national TV that he was working on a proposal to adapt the FEHBP model to some form of universal coverage.

These voices, covering most of the political spectrum, are advocating good ideas. Meanwhile, OPM has quite properly reacted in horror to the idea, advanced by some, that the FEHBP would directly enroll private workers in the same premium pool as Federal workers.

I suggest that serious consideration be given to the idea of using not only the FEHBP model, but also the existing FEHBP program, to advance private (and public) health insurance coverage.

Lest I be misunderstood, I am in no way suggesting that non-Federal workers would be enrolled in the FEHBP program itself. Any contract with OPM itself, or with FEHBP-participating plans such as GEHA or Kaiser HMO would be a separate contract with complete separation of finances and accounting.

However, why not offer the full panoply of existing FEHBP services to other public or private employers and plan sponsors at a reasonable charge? OPM could market:

- an experienced staff,
- Open Season and plan payment procedures in place,
- a set of plans that are known to be solvent and competent,
- a set of plan benefits that for the most part preempt state and local insurance mandates,
- a set of benefits that have been agreed and time tested as enrollee friendly,
- a set of plain English brochures that would apply to any payer with minor editing,
- and much more, all incorporated in a functioning system of plan choice.

The clients could be:

- employers large enough to handle premium collection and transfer
- states wanting to use the FEHBP rather than Medicaid model for the Child Health Insurance Program,
- multi-state companies wanting to piggyback on a better system than the ones devised by human resources staff or to avoid state mandates,
- municipalities frustrated at their inability to manage the complex process of health plan sponsorship at reasonable cost,
- trade associations wanting a good program for their members in all 50 states, or
- groups of displaced workers with tax credit assistance under the new Trade Adjustment Act.

Under such an authority, OPM would require that the premiums--both employer and employee share--be collected by a third party, guaranteed by bond, and transferred to OPM and then to participating plans just as OPM now handles retired workers. Individual plans could elect to decline to participate in third party systems. Total premium levels would either be those already negotiated by OPM or (as would be needed for children's insurance) those premiums subjected to actuarial adjustments. The balance between employer and employee premium shares would be determined by each client.

OPM has actually operated such an FEHBP-based system. The recently concluded DOD-FEHBP Demonstration project involved a separate premium structure, non-civil service enrollees, and plan-by-plan elections as to participation. While the demonstration project as designed was doomed to fail (and intended by the DOD health care establishment to fail) as an alternative to Tricare, it did in fact demonstrate that OPM can readily administer an FEHBP-like program for an alternative population.

As further insulation for OPM's primary responsibility as a service agency to the Federal civilian workforce, program sponsorship could be placed in the Department of Labor, which would contract with both OPM and private and public clients to provide this array of services.

I advance this idea, which would of course require careful analysis and legislative crafting, because it illustrates the potential for low-risk expansion of the FEHBP model in the simplest possible way. Why not export the FEHBP, while creating a tidy profit center for OPM, as a government service available for sale to the private sector? This would demonstrate the power of a multi-plan free market system whose detailed design decisions are made by the clients and service providers themselves, rather than by public or private bureaucratic fiat. If properly designed and insulated from the FEHBP itself, it would not in any way diminish or compromise the job that OPM performs for Federal civilian employees and annuitants, while providing a national demonstration of ideas and approaches endorsed by thoughtful analysts of every political persuasion.

Even though the finances of the program would be insulated from those of the $27 billion FEHBP program, the program would benefit from the increased willingness of participating plans to hold down premium levels to obtain additional business.

Conclusion. None of the reforms discussed above need disadvantage enrollees in the short run. All will benefit enrollees in the long run, by holding down unnecessary spending and reducing premium costs. If some of these reforms are not made, the FEHBP is likely to see costs surge over time. I urge the Congress to think "out of the box" in assessing the current state of the FEHBP and possible reform options like these. There is plenty of practical and analytic help to be found in the CBO, OMB, GAO, and OPM itself. The current OPM Director has shown herself more than willing to consider innovation and change. I wish you success in the coming session of Congress in making needed reforms to this vital program. It is not aging well.

Sources:

Dorn, Stan and Jack A. Meyer. 2002. *Nine Billion Dollars a Year to Cover the Uninsured: Possible Common Ground for Significant, Incremental Progress.* Washington DC. Economic and Social Research Institute. At www.esresearch.org.

Enthoven, Alain. "Where Are Health Care's 'Hondas'?" The Wall Street Journal. October 24, 2002.

Francis, Walton. 1993a. "The Political Economy of the Federal Employees Health Benefits Program." *Health Policy Reform: Competition and Controls*, edited by Robert B. Helms. Washington DC. AEI Press.

Francis, Walton. 1993b. "A Health Care Program Run by the Federal Government That Works." *The American Enterprise* magazine Volume 4, Number 4. Washington DC.

Francis,Walton. 1999. "FEHBP as a Model for Reform." *Medicare in the Twenty-first Century*, edited by Robert B. Helms. Washington DC. AEI Press.

Francis, Walton. 2002. "Premium Costs and Taxes". *CHECKBOOK's Guide to Health Plans for Federal Employees.* Washington, DC. Washington Consumers Checkbook. Retiree version and chapter text at www.retireehealthplans.org.

Hoff, John. 1998. *Medicare Private Contracting: Paternalism or Autonomy?* Washington, DC. AEI Press.

Joyce, Geoffrey et al. 2002. "Employer Drug Benefit Plans and Spending on Prescription Drugs." JAMA Volume 288, No. 14 (October 9, 2002).

Martinez, Barbara. 2002. "Health Benefits Post Highest Gain in Costs Since '90." *The Wall Street Journal.* December 9, 2002, page A6.

Moffit, Robert. 2001. *How Washington Can Improve Health Care Coverage for Federal Workers and Their Families.* Heritage Foundation, No. 1504. November 19, 2001. At www.heritage.org/library/backgrounder/bg1504.html.

U.S. Congressional Research Service. 1989. *The Federal Employees Health Benefits Program: Possible Strategies for Reform.* Washington, DC. Government Printing Office.

Mr. WELDON. Our next witness is recognized. Did I pronounce your name correctly? Is it Midgett?

Mr. MIDGETT. Mr. Chairman, members of the subcommittee and other individuals and organizations interested in the health benefits of postal and Federal employees and retirees, I am testifying before you today on behalf of Mr. William Burrus, president of the American Postal Workers Union, its 260,000 members, and enrollees of the APWU health plan. We are truly honored by this invitation to testify on the subject of recent developments in the Federal Employees Health Benefits system.

The APWU health plan covers 120,000 people and has been part of the FEHBP program since its inception over 40 years ago. We are extremely proud of our record of providing protection and service to our members and their families throughout these many years. In your letter of invitation, the subcommittee has specifically asked us to address the decision to offer a new consumer-driven option for 2003 and the evolution of that product's development, so that will be the focus of my testimony today.

Although the APWU health plan is still today one of the largest health plans participating in the FEHBP program, the membership under its Single High Option has been declining steadily, though not dramatically, over recent years. In order to remain competitive over time and continue to be a benefit to the union that sponsors it, the plan determined that it needed to explore a new offering in addition to its existing High Option. Observing membership trends among other FEHBP fee-for-service plans convinced us that only marginal results can be achieved by introducing a Standard Plan Option with a similar benefit designed to our High Option, but with higher deductibles and catastrophic limits in exchange for a lower premium.

We began looking for alternative benefit designs to evaluate health insurance products that might be attractive and price competitive for members of the APWU who are not being drawn to our High Option for whatever reasons. Over the past year we began following a new concept in the health care industry called consumer-driven health care. It seemed to be enjoying increasing popularity in the private sector.

We felt that this product had features that would be attractive to members of the American Postal Workers Union and to others as well. It was certainly innovative and the departure from any benefit design offered through the FEHBP program. Among the features we found attractive were the concept of the personal care account, a first-dollar, 100 percent benefit almost entirely under the consumer's control, unused benefits which could be rolled over into subsequent years.

We also liked the underlying concept of placing the consumer in control of their health care decisions while providing incentives for wise decisionmaking, and furnishing the consumer with the tools and resources necessary to enable them to make effective decisions.

Simply, this design puts the onus on the individual to shop wisely for health care services, rather than the insurance company, to try to manage their care for them. The result is a new level of consumer freedom that rewards the consumer for making wise, cost-conscious decisions.

Clearly, the APWU health plan could not develop claims processing systems and a full range of Internet-based consumer resources to self-administer this type of product in so short a time and, therefore, had to seek a firm capable of administering the product for us. With the assistance of our actuarial consultants, we issued a request for proposal to firms already experienced in offering consumer-driven health care. After thorough analysis of bids, we selected Definity Health of Minneapolis, Minnesota, as our partner, based on a combination of factors including administrative costs, product flexibility, and education assistance.

A collaborative effort between the APWU health plan, its actuarial consultants, Definity Health plan and, later, staff at the U.S. Office of Personnel Management refined and customized the offering of APWU's proposal and introduction into the FEHBP program.

In the APWU health plan's consumer-driven option for 2003 there are four components. First, to ensure that everyone has access to necessary preventive care, there is an in-network preventive care benefit which covers specified routine examinations, immunizations, and screenings at 100 percent and does not count against the second component, the personal care account, or PCA.

The PCA really sets the consumer-driven option apart from other conventional health plan designs. Under our plan, the PCA is used to pay for the first $1,000 for an individual enrollment, or $2,000 for a family enrollment, in full for covered services including dental and vision care up to specified limits. Any unused PCA benefits may be rolled over into the next year.

If the PCA is exhausted, consumers pay a member responsibility of $600 for an individual or $1,200 for a family enrollment. Once the member responsibility is met, the traditional health coverage begins. This traditional health coverage is a PPO plan with cost-sharing and catastrophic protection. Extensive Internet-based tools and resources are offered to consumers to help them make wise cost and quality decisions about their health care. The same tools and resources are also available via the telephone as well.

The APWU health plan's consumer-driven option offers consumers more flexibility and choices in managing their health care and also helps contain health care costs by involving the consumer in the health care equation through a comparative cost awareness.

In soliciting health plan proposals for 2003, the Director of OPM specifically has plans to come to the table with innovative ideas that will keep health care costs affordable while offering a benefit program that will be attractive to current employees and retirees, as well as prospective Federal employees, which is consistent with the President's vision of health care, patient-centered health care, choice, and quality.

The APWU health plan believes that its decision to offer this new consumer-driven option is absolutely appropriate and timely in addressing these objectives and in providing an innovative, new, cost-effective choice for our existing and prospective members.

I have brought with me today Michael Showalter, the Vice President of Product Development from Definity Health care. At this time, we would be happy to respond to any questions that committee members might have. And thank you for your time and interest.

Mr. WELDON. Thank you very much.

[The prepared statement of Mr. Midgett follows:]

87-416 D-3

APWU HEALTH PLAN
PO Box 420, Burtonsville, MD 20866
American Postal Workers Union, AFL-CIO
Health Plan Department
Chief Operating Manager
Carroll E Midgett, Jr.
(301) 622-5554

Testimony of

CARROLL E. MIDGETT
CHIEF OPERATING MANAGER
APWU HEALTH PLAN

before the

Subcommittee on the Civil Service, Census and
Agency Organization
of the
Committee on Government Reform

Wednesday, December 11, 2002
Room 2247, Rayburn House Office Building

Testimony of
Carroll E. Midgett, Chief Operating Manager APWU Health Plan

Before

Subcommittee on the Civil Service, Census and Agency
Organization of the Committee on Government Reform
United States House of Representatives
Wednesday, December 11, 2002

Mr. Chairman, members of the Subcommittee and other individuals and organizations interested in the health benefits of Postal and Federal employees and retirees. I am testifying before you today on behalf of Mr. William Burrus, President of the American Postal Workers Union, AFL-CIO; its 360,000 members and the enrollees of its APWU Health Plan. We are truly honored by this invitation to testify on the subject of Recent Developments in the Federal Employees Health Benefits System.

The APWU Health Plan covers over 120,000 people and has been a part of the FEHB Program since its inception over 40 years ago. We are extremely proud of our record of providing protection and service to our members and their families throughout these many years. In your letter of invitation, the Subcommittee has specifically asked us to address the decision to offer a new Consumer-driven Option for 2003 and the evolution of that product's development so that will be the focus of my testimony today.

Although APWU Health Plan is still today one of the largest health plans participating in the FEHB Program, the membership under its single High Option plan has been declining steadily, though not dramatically, over recent years. It became apparent to the Union and its health plan management that consumer interests concerning their health benefits have been changing along with other commonly recognized factors that are impacting the program, namely an aging employee population and rising health care costs.

In order to remain competitive over time and continue to be a benefit to the Union that sponsors it, the Plan determined that it would have to explore the development of a new benefit offering in addition to the existing High Option. Observing membership trends among other FEHB fee-for-service plans convinced us that only marginal results could be achieved by introducing a standard option plan with a similar benefit design to our High Option but with higher deductibles and catastrophic limits in exchange for a lower premium. We began looking for alternative benefit designs to evaluate; health insurance products that might be attractive and price-competitive for members of the APWU who were not being drawn to our High Option for whatever reasons.

Over the past year, APWU Health Plan management began following a new concept in healthcare called Consumer-Driven Healthcare that seemed to be enjoying increasing popularity in the private sector. We felt that this product had a number of features that would be attractive to members of the APWU and to many other FEHB – eligible people, as well. It was certainly innovative and a departure from any benefit design previously offered through the FEHB Program. Among the general product features we found attractive were the concept of the Personal Care Account; a first-dollar, 100% benefit almost entirely under the consumers' control, unused benefits of which could be rolled over to subsequent years.

We also liked the underlying concept of placing the consumer in control of their healthcare decisions while providing incentives as motivation for wise decision-making and furnishing the consumer with the tools and resources necessary to enable them to make effective decisions. Simply, this design puts the onus on the individual to shop wisely for healthcare services rather than on the insurance carrier to try to manage their care for them. The result is a new level of consumer freedom that rewards the consumer for making wise, cost-conscious choices.

Clearly, APWU Health Plan could not develop claims processing systems and a full range of Internet-based consumer resources to self-administer this type of product in so short a time and, therefore, had to seek a firm capable of administering the product for us. With the assistance of our actuarial consultants, we issued a Request for Proposal (RFP) to firms that already had experience in offering Consumer – Driven HealthCare. After thorough analysis of bids, we selected Definity Health of Minneapolis, Minnesota as our partner based upon a combination of factors including administrative costs, product flexibility, and marketing assistance.

A collaborative effort between APWU Health Plan staff, its actuarial consultants, Definity Health staff and, later, staff at the U.S. Office of Personnel Management (OPM) refined and customized the offering for APWU's proposal and introduction to the FEHB Program.

In APWU Health Plan's Consumer-driven Option for 2003, there are four components.

First, to ensure that everyone has access to necessary preventive care, there is an In-network Preventive Care benefit which covers specified routine examinations, immunizations and screenings at 100% and does not count against the second component, the Personal Care Account, or PCA.

The PCA really sets the Consumer-driven Option apart from other conventional health plan designs. Under the APWU plan, the PCA is used to pay the first $1,000 per individual or $2,000 per family in full for covered services, including dental and vision care up to a specified limit. Any PCA benefits left unused may be rolled over to the next year and then in subsequent years up to a maximum rollover limit of $4,000 per individual or $6,000 per family.

If the personal care account is exhausted, consumers pay a Member Responsibility of $600 for an individual or $1200 for a family. Once the Member Responsibility is met, their Traditional Health Coverage begins. Traditional Health Coverage is a traditional Preferred Provider Organization (PPO) plan with traditional cost sharing (plan pays 85% in-network and 60% out-of-network) with a Catastrophic Protection limit. Extensive Internet-based tools and resources are offered to consumers to help them make wise cost and quality decisions about their health care. The same tools and resources are available by telephone, as well. APWU Health Plan's Consumer-driven Option offers consumers more flexibility and choices in managing their health care, and also helps contain health care costs by involving consumers in the health care equation through comparative cost awareness.

In soliciting health plan proposals for 2003, the Director of OPM specifically asked plans to come to the table with innovative ideas that will help keep health care costs affordable while offering a benefit program that will be attractive to current employees and retirees, as well as to prospective Federal employees and which are consistent with the President's vision for health care; patient-centered health care, choice and quality. APWU Health Plan believes that its decision to offer this new Consumer-driven Option is absolutely appropriate and timely in addressing these objectives and in providing an innovative new, cost-effective choice for our members and others eligible for FEHB benefits.

At this time, we would be happy to respond to any questions the committee members might have and we thank you for your time and interest.

Mr. WELDON. We will now hear testimony from Ms. Kelley. You are recognized for 5 minutes.

Ms. KELLEY. Thank you, Chairman Weldon, Ranking Member Davis. NTEU very much appreciates the invitation to appear before you today to discuss these important issues surrounding the FEHBP plan.

The average 11 percent premium increase for 2003 marks the fifth year in a row for steep increases in the plan. To the extent that Federal employees are finding the FEHBP increasingly not affordable, and prospective employees consider this, it is an issue that we all must deal with and we cannot afford to ignore.

While FEHBP plans are increasing their premiums, they are often also increasing their copayments and deductibles, limiting services, dropping participating physicians and increasing prescription drug copays. In addition, HMOs are dropping out and limiting their offerings in certain parts of the country.

While health insurance premiums have risen dramatically in the private sector, private-sector employees continue to pay, on an average, considerably less than Federal employees for their health insurance in terms of both percentage of premiums that they pay, as well as their monthly cost.

The Kaiser 2002 Annual Survey of Employer Health Benefits reports that the average private-sector employee pays $38 per month for single coverage and $174 a month for family coverage. In 2003, a Federal employee choosing Blue Cross/Blue Shield Standard Option, Self Only, will pay $98.93 per month, instead of the $38 paid in the private sector; and the Federal employee choosing Blue Cross Standard, Family coverage, will pay $227.98 a month.

This sharp contrast continues when we look at the percentage of the premiums that employees pay. As has already been discussed, Federal employees pay, on the average, 28 percent of their health insurance premiums. And the Kaiser study points out that, on average, employees in the private sector pay only 16 percent of the premium for Self Only coverage and 27 percent for Family coverage.

NTEU supports H.R. 1307, introduced by Congressman Steny Hoyer and cosponsored by 94 House Members in the 107th Congress, seeking to increase the government's coverage to an average of 80 percent. NTEU hopes that this subcommittee will consider the bill when it is reintroduced next year and place the Federal Government on a somewhat more level playing field with private-sector employees, both for current employees and for potential employees of the Federal Government.

NTEU worked very closely with the last administration to put the premium conversion in place to permit employees to pay their FEHBP premiums with before-tax wages. The average Federal employee saves $450 in take-home pay. This was a very positive development for current and for potential employees. NTEU is also pleased that the current administration will make flexible spending accounts available to the Federal work force in late 2003, allowing employees to set aside a specific amount of money to pay health care and independent care expenses on a pretax basis. The savings can be considerable for employees.

Unfortunately, retirees are not currently permitted to participate in either program, and NTEU supports extending these key health care cost-reducing benefits to retired Federal employees.

On the issue of MSAs, as NTEU has testified in the past, we have serious concerns about these or similar insurance products entering into the FEHBP. These products have the potential to add considerable cost to the Federal health program. They tend to attract younger, healthier enrollees, who have minimal health care, with cash. Those with higher utilization levels tend to be left in the traditional health offerings, and as a result, the premiums for those traditional health plans rise.

While I recognize that the new APWU plan is not an MSA, its introduction into the FEHBP and its potential impact on future rates is cause for concern. Like MSAs, this consumer-driven plan is expected to be most attractive to younger and healthier FEHBP enrollees. The impact of this plan on future rates is obviously unknown at this time, but NTEU wants to make the subcommittee aware of our concerns, and we will be watching the usage and the growth in this plan carefully.

Finally, I want to point out that one of the largest factors in FEHBP premium increases has been prescription drug costs. The patchwork of prescription drug purchase arrangements in the FEHBP contributes to these increases. NTEU believes that OPM must negotiate discount prescription drug rates for the FEHBP that are similar to those available under the Federal supply schedule and that are used by the Veterans Administration hospitals.

As you know, in 1999, one small FEHBP plan attempted to purchase its drugs from the Federal supply schedule. Unfortunately, the plan which is SAMBA, the Special Agents Mutual Benefit Association, was halted when three major pharmaceutical companies refused to sell drugs to SAMBA if they were permitted to purchase drugs from the FSS. The SAMBA pilot had been estimated to save $2.4 million a year, savings that would have flowed to Federal employees, to retirees, and to taxpayers.

The idea behind the SAMBA pilot continues to merit exploration. At a minimum, NTEU believes that OPM should be encouraged to study the merits in negotiating discount prescription drug rates for the FEHBP.

Again, NTEU appreciates this opportunity to appear before you, and we look forward to working with you and the 108th Congress on this issue.

Mr. WELDON. Thank you very much.

[The prepared statement of Ms. Kelley follows:]

Testimony Of

Colleen M. Kelley

National President

National Treasury Employees Union

on

The Federal Employees Health Benefits Program

December 11, 2002

11:00 AM

Civil Service Subcommittee
Committee on Government Reform
2247 Rayburn Building

Chairman Weldon, Ranking Member Davis, Members of the Subcommittee, my name is Colleen M. Kelley and I am the National President of the National Treasury Employees Union (NTEU). NTEU represents more than 150,000 federal employees across 28 agencies and departments of the federal government.

We very much appreciate being invited to appear before your Subcommittee today to share our thoughts on the many issues facing the Federal Employees Health Benefits Program (FEHBP). The annual FEHBP Open Season, which concluded earlier this week, ushered in several changes in the federal health program, several of which are of great concern to NTEU and its members.

As you know, the average 11.1% premium increase for 2003 marks the fifth year in a row of exorbitant rate increases in the federal health program. The 2002 rate increase averaged 13.3%. For 2001 the increase was 10.5%; in 2000 it was 9.3% and in 1999, 9.5%. As you also know, federal employee salary increases have not kept pace with these rate hikes, forcing many participating employees -

as well as retirees - to closely examine whether or not they can afford to continue in the program. To the extent federal employees are finding the FEHBP increasingly unaffordable and prospective employees are discouraged from seeking employment with the federal government as a result of the health program's costs, this is an issue none of us can afford to ignore.

For 2003, six of the seven participating FEHBP fee-for-service plans that are open to all employees and retirees raised their premiums. However, this doesn't even begin to tell the full story of the costs employees and retirees are faced with. At the same time plans are increasing their premiums, they are often simultaneously increasing their required copayments and deductibles, limiting their covered services, dropping participating physicians from their programs and increasing the amount of prescription drug copays that enrollees must pay out of pocket.

Moreover, eleven participating Health Maintenance Organizations (HMOs) dropped out of the program for 2003, several more have curtailed their offerings in certain parts of the country and still others have reduced the service areas in which they operate.

While health insurance premiums have risen dramatically in the private sector in recent years as well, it is important to point out that private sector employees continue to pay, on average, less for their health insurance - both in terms of percentage of premium and in terms of monthly cost - than their federal counterparts.

The respected Kaiser Family Foundation's 2002 Annual Survey of Employer Health Benefits reports that, "on average employees are now paying $38 per month ($454 per year) for single coverage," and "$174 per month ($2,084 per year) for family coverage." The differences between average private sector monthly premiums and the monthly amounts federal employees pay for the most popular FEHBP plan are startling.

For 2003, a federal employee choosing Blue Cross-Blue Shield Standard Option Self Only coverage will pay $98.93 each month, or $1,187.16 annually. An employee choosing family coverage under Blue Cross Standard Option will pay $227.98 each month for this coverage, or $2,735.76.

This sharp contrast continues when we look at the percentage of premium employees are required to absorb. The federal government currently pays an average of 72% of the health insurance premium for its employees. Yet, the Kaiser study points out that on average, employees in the private sector are required to pay only 16% of premium for self only coverage and 27% for family coverage.

NTEU believes we have a responsibility to look at the impact these issues have had, and will continue to have, on the ability of the federal government to attract and retain employees. This same Kaiser study makes the impact in the private sector clear - it reports that employers who have passed along health insurance cost increases to their employees are feeling the effects with regard to their ability to attract and retain workers. Of the firms that increased the amount their employees must pay for health insurance coverage in 2002, Kaiser reports that 41% found that it was subsequently more difficult to attract and retain employees.

These factors have helped to form the basis of NTEU's support for legislation to increase the employer share of FEHBP premiums from the current average of 72% to 80%. As the Chairman knows, bipartisan legislation was introduced by Congressman Steny Hoyer in the 107th Congress to accomplish this important goal. Although the Subcommittee did not consider this legislation, H.R.1307 nonetheless was endorsed by 94 members of the House of Representatives.

NTEU anticipates that Congressman Hoyer will reintroduce this important legislation in the 108th Congress and we will work closely with his office to secure its passage. In addition, we hope that this Subcommittee will give the legislation early and fair consideration. By placing the federal government on somewhat more level ground with the private sector employers with which it competes, H.R.1307 represents a key first step in insuring that the federal government will be able to compete now and in the future for the talent it needs.

Over the years, NTEU has pressed for other improvements in the federal benefit package that we believe are central to recruiting and retaining the best employees. For example, we worked closely with the last Administration to put in place a mechanism to permit federal employees to pay their FEHBP premiums with before-tax wages. Called Premium Conversion, it is a benefit private sector employers have offered to their employees since 1978. While the federal government did not make Premium Conversion Accounts available to its employees until 2000, NTEU is nonetheless grateful that federal employees are finally able to take advantage of the benefits Premium Conversion offers.

NTEU believes that the extension of this benefit throughout the federal sector enhances the ability of the federal government to compete in the labor market. Moreover, the average federal employee has experienced a $450 annual increase in take home pay as a result of Premium Conversion. Hopefully, this will also help those employees unable to afford FEHBP coverage to be better able to purchase it.

NTEU is also pleased that the current Administration has agreed to make full Flexible Spending Accounts (FSAs) available to the federal workforce in mid-2003. Like Premium Conversion Accounts, FSAs have been available to private sector workers for many years. An employee eligible for an FSA account sets aside a specific amount of money each year to pay certain health care and dependent care expenses on a pre-tax basis. Qualifying expenses include out-of-pocket medical expenses such as copayments and deductibles, routine physicals and immunizations that may not be covered by insurance, braces, vision exams, eyeglasses and even child and elder care expenses.

The savings associated with FSAs can be considerable. An employee in the Civil Service Retirement System (CSRS) who is in the 15% tax bracket and sets aside $2,000 in an FSA account for medical and dependent care expenses can expect savings of more than $420 annually. An employee in the 15% income tax bracket who participates in the Federal Employees Retirement System (FERS) and also sets aside $2,000 in an FSA account can expect to save $550 annually.

As the Chairman also knows, however, only current federal employees are permitted to participate in Premium Conversion. Under current law, federal retirees will also be excluded from participation in Flexible Spending Accounts. NTEU strongly supports extending these key health care cost reducing benefits to retired federal employees and urges this Subcommittee to look carefully at these issues in the next Congress. Congressman Tom Davis introduced H.R.2125 in the 107th Congress and although it was not acted upon before the Congress' conclusion, I expect that it will be reintroduced early in 2003. I urge its favorable consideration.

As NTEU has made clear in past testimony, we have serious reservations about the introduction of Medical Savings Accounts (MSAs), or similar insurance products, into the FEHBP. These products have the potential to add dramatic costs to the federal health program. MSAs tend to attract younger, healthier enrollees and reward lower health care usage with cash balances. Less healthy and older health care enrollees tend to be left in the traditional health offerings. As a result, the premiums for those traditional health plans rise. This is precisely the fear the Congressional Budget Office (CBO) expressed when it estimated that adding MSAs to the FEHBP would increase federal spending by almost $1 billion over five years.

While I recognize that the new American Postal Workers Union (APWU) plan is not an MSA, its introduction into the FEHBP family and its potential impact on future rate stability are cause for concern. Much like an MSA, this "Consumer-Driven Plan" is expected to be most attractive to younger and healthier FEHBP enrollees.

FEHBP participants signing up for APWU's new Consumer-Driven Plan will be provided with a health care spending account worth $1,000 for individuals and $2,000 for families. Enrollees can use this money for almost any health-related service, however, once the money has been spent, the next $600 (or $1,200 for families) of care must come directly from the enrollees' pocket. Only after this level of health care spending has been reached will the plan begin to pay 85% of in-network health care services and 60% of out-of-network care. If the enrollee does not spend all of the $1,000 (or $2,000 for family enrollment) in his or her health care spending account, the money can be carried forward to the next plan year - assuming the enrollee does not opt out of the Consumer-Driven Plan during the next open season.

Simply put, the plan rewards enrollees with either cash balances or extra health care coverage for not using medical care. Siphoning off healthy FEHBP participants while leaving those with higher utilization levels in the traditional plans seems to defy the underlying principle of group health insurance by separating these two groups of individuals. The impact of this plan on future FEHBP rates is obviously not known at this time, however, NTEU wants to make sure the Subcommittee is aware of our serious concerns.

Finally, Mr. Chairman, I want to point out that one of the largest factors in the rise in FEHBP premiums over the years has been prescription drug costs. There is little question that the patchwork of prescription drug purchase arrangements that exists in the FEHBP contributes to these annual increases. NTEU continues to believe that the Office of Personnel Management must negotiate discount prescription drug rates for the FEHBP similar to those available under the Federal Supply Schedule (FSS) used by Veterans Administration hospitals.

As you may recall, in 1999, one small FEHBP plan attempted to purchase its drugs from the FSS. Unfortunately, the Special Agents Mutual Benefit Association's (SAMBA) proposal was thwarted when three major pharmaceutical companies - Pfizer, Merck and Parke-Davis refused to sell drugs to SAMBA if they were permitted to purchase drugs from the FSS.

Although this pilot project would have resulted in a minuscule loss of profit to these three major drug companies and would have provided valuable data on whether or not OPM's development of a similar drug schedule for the FEHBP would help reign in drug costs in the program, the pilot was not permitted to go forward.

The SAMBA pilot had been estimated to save $2.4 million a year, savings that would have flowed to federal employees and retirees as well as to taxpayers. Although the pharmaceutical industry has thus far prevented the FEHBP from as much as even examining the value of creating such a drug schedule for use by FEHBP plans, the idea continues to merit exploration. At a minimum, NTEU believes that the Office of Personnel Management should be encouraged to study the merits of negotiating discount prescription drug rates for the FEHBP and hopes that this Subcommittee will work with them to this end.

In conclusion, Mr. Chairman, NTEU certainly appreciates this opportunity to appear before you. We very much look forward to working with you in the 108th Congress on the key issues facing the FEHBP that we have outlined here today. Thank you.

Mr. WELDON. Mr. Fallis, you are recognized for 5 minutes.

Mr. FALLIS. Chairman Weldon, Ranking Member Davis, I appreciate the opportunity to come before you today and speak on behalf of the 400,000 members of NARFE.

We in NARFE were disturbed by the Office of Personnel Management's announcement that the FEHBP premiums would increase by an average of 11 percent next year. However, we understand that costly rate increases are not unique to our plan and that other systems are experiencing even greater spikes. The reality is that most of the retirees average monthly COLA of $26 in 2003 will be consumed by these premium increases which will take effect next year, and that will leave many of our members and many of our retirees in dire straits.

To lessen the burden of the premium increases, section 125 of the Tax Code allows employers to permit their employees to pay for health insurance with wages excluded from taxes. This premium conversion benefit was granted to executive branch employees in October 2000 and was extended also to legislative branch employees in January 2001. Unfortunately, Federal annuitants were excluded from the program since the Tax Code was less clear on making premium conversion benefits available to retirees. As a matter of equity, however, Federal annuitants must be accorded this same relief.

NARFE welcomed the premium conversion legislation introduced by Representative Tom Davis and Senator John Warner in the 107th Congress. This legislation, if passed, would have meant about a $405 savings per year for the retiree. We urge you, Mr. Chairman, and you, Mr. Davis and the members of this subcommittee, to renew your support for premium conversion legislation and seek its speedy consideration and approval in the 108th Congress.

NARFE has made premium conversion a top priority. Because of the burden borne by the Federal annuitants and employees, NARFE supports and will continue to support legislation introduced by Congressman Hoyer that would increase the government contribution from 72 to 80 percent of the weighted average of all planned premiums.

NARFE is disturbed by the decisions of the American Postal Workers Union and the OPM to offer a so-called customer- or a consumer-driven option for 2003. Medical savings accounts, which NARFE strongly opposes, are plans that combine a high deductible catastrophic insurance policy with a tax-exempt savings account dedicated for health expenses. Although the personal care account component of the APWU plan is not tax exempt and provides credits toward health care instead of cash, there is little or nothing to distinguish this option from an MSA.

These expensive financing schemes can be attractive to the healthier enrollees since the plans reward them with either increasing cash balances or extra coverage carried forward in subsequent years if they don't go to a doctor or if they don't go to a hospital. As a result, healthy individuals are siphoned into the new option and premiums, and the comprehensive plans they left will inevitably be increased. Consequently, MSAs and related plans could circumvent the fundamental principles of group health insurance by dividing the healthy and the sick into separate coverage options.

We are hopeful that future announcements do not include using new health reimbursement accounts with high deductible health insurance as a proxy for offering MSAs. Likewise, while we support making flexible savings accounts available to Federal annuitants, we are concerned that they could also be used as an MSA substitute if legislation is enacted to allow FSA balances to be rolled over.

It is simply a mistake to transform a successful group health system where risk-sharing keeps health insurance affordable and predictable throughout life to an every-man-for-himself scheme where premiums and out-of-pocket expenses are reasonable only for healthy participants. For 42 years the Federal Employees Health Benefits program has minimized costs and provided a wide choice of comprehensive health insurance plans to nearly 9 million Federal employees, retirees and their families.

NARFE stands ready to work with all parties to find ways and means of containing out-of-control health care costs, but without sacrificing quality, access and coverage and without eliminating risk-sharing in this largest group plan environment.

Thank you, Mr. Chairman.

Mr. WELDON. Thank you very much, Mr. Fallis for your testimony.

[The prepared statement of Mr. Fallis follows:]

STATEMENT BY
CHARLES L. FALLIS
PRESIDENT
NATIONAL ASSOCIATION OF RETIRED FEDERAL EMPLOYEES

TO THE SUBCOMMITTEE ON CIVIL SERVICE
COMMITTEE ON
GOVERNMENT REFORM AND OVERSIGHT
U.S. HOUSE OF REPRESENTATIVES

HEARING ON
FEDERAL EMPLOYEES HEALTH BENEFITS PROGRAM (FEHBP)

DECEMBER 11, 2002

Mr. Chairman, on behalf of the 400,000 member National Association of Retired Federal Employees (NARFE), we appreciate the opportunity to express our views on the 2003 rate increase for the Federal Employees Health Benefits Program (FEHBP) and other recent developments in the program.

Like others in the federal community, we were disturbed by the Office of Personnel Management's (OPM) announcement that FEHBP premiums would increase by an average of 11 percent next year. Federal annuitants will be particularly hard hit by the 2003 premium increases because their annuity cost- of- living adjustment (COLA) was only 1.4 percent, and because they have had to absorb significant rate hikes during the previous four years.

While providing little comfort to our members, we understand that costly FEHBP premium increases are not unique to FEHBP and that other large employer-sponsored health insurance systems are experiencing even greater spikes. For instance, the California Public Employees Retirement System (CALPERS) health plan, second only in size to FEHBP, will increase premiums by an average of 25 percent in 2003.

Although the average FEHBP premium increase in 2003 will be 11 percent, the consulting firm Watson Wyatt found in a survey of large employer-sponsored health insurance plans that average premium costs increased by 13.6 percent for employees and 15.1 percent for Medicare-covered retirees this year. Another reputable employee benefits consulting firm -- Hewitt Associates – projects that its clients will pay an average premium increase of 15.4 percent in 2003. NARFE commends OPM Director Kay Coles James and her health benefits staff for keeping most FEHBP premiums below these national averages.

As we see it, there are several reasons why high care costs have spiked during the past few years.

First, the cost containment features and efficiencies of managed care plans -- like health maintenance organizations (HMOs) -- have proven to be temporary, as many had warned. Indeed, this has been particularly true regarding managed care's diminished ability to constrain payment rates and use of hospital services. In FEHBP, managed care plans will increase premiums by 13.6 percent next year while fee-for-service options will match the program-wide average increase of 10.5 percent. No doubt savings have been "squeezed" out of the program – but at what cost to the federal family? We were heartened by the preservation of choice in FEHBP but implore you not to waver in your vigilance to provide quality benefits in order to recruit and retain employees and to fulfill the promise of deferred compensation in federal employment.

Although FEHBP premiums have increased in previous years because the program serves an aging community of both employees and retirees, the effect of age on rates has become relatively small. According to the Office of Personnel Management (OPM), age and other demographic sources only contributed to 0.7 percent of the 2003 average premium increase. Health care economists Bradley C. Strunk and Paul B. Ginsburg recently found that the aging U.S. population was only responsible for 0.7 percent of the increase in medical expenses last year.

Like other health plans, the skyrocketing cost of prescription drugs has significantly contributed to higher insurance premiums. Several years ago, drug costs accounted for less than 10 percent of health plan expenses. Today, that amount has increased to 25 percent of insurance benefits in FEHBP. According to the Milliman USA Health Care Index (HCI), prescription drug costs rose 13.8 percent in 2001 and accounted for 21 percent of new health care costs last year.

Most health policy analysts agree that prescription drug use has risen because there are more pharmaceuticals available today that sustain or improve the quality of life. However, direct industry-to-consumer marketing of new drugs has also influenced increased utilization. In fact, drug companies spend as much as 35 cents of every dollar of revenue on marketing.

According to the nonpartisan Congressional Research Service (CRS), the pharmaceutical industry in recent years has earned about 18 cents after taxes for every dollar of revenue, or three times the rate of the average U.S. company.

While rising drug costs account for a significant portion of the 70 percent increase in FEHBP premiums since 1998, utilization, technology and medical inflation contributed a larger share to both the 2002 and 2003 rate hikes. Specifically, hospital spending resulted in more than half of the growth in total U.S. health care spending according to "Tracking Health Care Costs: Growth Accelerates Again in 2001" in the September 2002 *Health Affairs*. The articles authors' Strunk,

Ginsburg and Jon R. Gabel explain that "over the past few years hospitals have regained a sizable amount of negotiating leverage over health plans and have used it to demand large payment increases." Significant growth in the use of hospital services also has been added to the spike in this category of health care spending.

Lessening the Burden

Section 125 of the Internal Revenue Code presently allows employers in the public and private sectors to permit their employees to pay for health insurance with wages excluded from both income and Social Security payroll taxes. President Clinton offered this "premium conversion" benefit to federal employees in October 2000 through Section 125. According to OPM, the average federal worker saves about $434 a year by lowering their taxable income by the amount of an employee's health care premium. These so-called "premium conversion plans" are available to many employees of large private-sector companies.

However, federal annuitants were excluded from the program since tax code authority to make premium conversion benefits available to retirees is less clear. As a matter of equity, federal annuitants must receive this same relief. Annuitants live on fixed incomes, and much of the 1.3 to 3.5 percent COLAs received by federal annuitants and military retirees during the last five years have been eroded by double-digit increases in health insurance premiums.

We appreciate that the members of this panel understand that -- at an average monthly annuity of $1,869 -- most federal retirees and survivors -- while not poverty stricken – are not living in the lap of luxury either. The reality is that most of the average monthly COLA of $26.00 in 2003 will be consumed by FEHBP enrollee share increases, like the $22.52 jump in the Blue Cross/Blue Shield standard option family plan.

NARFE supported legislation introduced by Representative Tom Davis and Senator John Warner during the 107th Congress, to allow federal annuitants to use pre-tax annuities to pay their share of FEHBP premiums. Federal annuitants with family FEHBP plans could save an average of $405 a year on their income taxes if federal annuitants were allowed to pay premiums with pre-tax dollars. Military retirees also would be permitted to pay their share of TRICARE premiums with pre-tax retirement pay under the Davis and Warner bills. We urge you, Mr. Chairman, and members of the subcommittee, to support premium conversion legislation and to seek its speedy consideration and approval in the 108th Congress.

We understand that some of your colleagues have expressed concerns that premium conversion would be extended only to federal and military retirees – and not other retirees – under the proposed legislation. Because of our devotion to public service, NARFE suggests that providing the premium conversion to federal and military retirees is a reasonable first step toward providing it to all retirees.

If fully implemented, the Joint Committee on Taxation says that premium conversion legislation would cost $7.1 billion over ten years. Some of your colleagues have asked how we justify spending that much money. In response, we have said that several proposals to use the tax code to help other Americans absorb skyrocketing health care costs have received -- and are likely to continue to receive -- favorable consideration. The cost of premium conversion legislation is not out of line with other plans presently under consideration.

Some here on Capitol Hill have also asked us why is it necessary to extend the Section 125 premium conversion benefit to federal and military retirees when the same thing could be accomplished if we provide them wit an above-the-line tax deduction for their share of health insurance premiums. NARFE has reminded them that a tax savings is achieved by the premium conversion benefit because the participant's income reported by their employer to the Internal Revenue Service (IRS) is reduced by the amount they pay in health insurance premiums. Consequently, a retiree or her accountant would not be required to itemize or complete any special forms. Indeed, their taxes would be reduced because their taxable income is reduced. It simply makes it easier, especially for older retirees or those who are incapacitated to receive this tax relief automatically

The burden borne by federal annuitants and employees would have also been reduced by H.R. 1307, legislation introduced by Representative Steny Hoyer that would have increased the government contribution from 72 to 80 percent of the weighted average of all FEHBP plan premiums. Many employers contribute a larger share than the federal government for their employees' premiums. [In 2001 and 2002, for example, employees paid about 15.5 percent of self-only plan premiums and 27.3 percent for family plans.[1]] Increasing the FEHBP employer share would help the federal government attract the best and the brightest to public service.

[1] "Tracking Health Care Costs: Growth Accelerates Again in 2001", September 2002, *Health Affairs, by* Bradley C. Strunk, Paul B. Ginsburg and Jon R. Gabel.

Containing Costs

In addition, NARFE supported the Special Agents Mutual Benefit Association (SAMBA) prescription drug demonstration program that was canceled by OPM in 2000 due to the pharmaceutical industry's refusal to participate in the project. The pilot project would have allowed SAMBA to buy certain drugs for its enrollees at the discount mandated by the federal supply schedule (FSS), a procurement tool used by the Department of Defense and Veterans Administration health care systems. NARFE was disappointed that some major pharmaceutical companies refused to play a role in a modest proposal to contain high drug costs for working families, retirees living on fixed incomes and the taxpayers. We were also troubled by the opposition of some FEHBP insurance carriers to the SAMBA demonstration while the same firms seemed to be less concerned about shifting new costs to enrollees.

Beyond the SAMBA demonstration, NARFE continues to be interested in discussing other ways to contain prescription drug costs with this panel and the OPM. For instance, some FEHBP plans use pharmaceutical benefit managers (PBMs) to lower or contain drug costs by negotiating discounts with pharmaceutical manufacturers. Indeed, some of the Medicare drug benefit proposals considered this year would employ PBMs.

NARFE supports enhancing the ability of pharmaceutical benefit managers to leverage the federal community's large economy of scale when negotiating drug discounts with the pharmaceutical industry.

Enhanced PBM leverage also could be complemented if the OPM, federal employee and annuitant organizations, and FEHBP carriers joined together in educating enrollees about the benefits of using generic drugs -- specifically, that generic drugs, when available, are almost always a medically appropriate substitute to name brands and that greater use of generics could result in significant savings for participants and taxpayers. We also support additional efforts to remove statutory and regulatory roadblocks that some pharmaceutical manufactures use to needlessly delay the availability of generic drugs.

Quality, Coverage and Access vs. Cost Containment

In an environment of double digit premium increases, our members support innovative methods of reining in out-of-control health care costs in FEHBP. At the same time, however, most federal annuitants and workers would prefer to retain the ability to select their own physicians, specialists and other providers under their current fee-for-service plans. For that reason, we have concerns about any plan that attempts to reduce access to providers and facilities. That is why NARFE supported the February 1998 executive order that required FEHBP carriers to provide access to specialists and emergency room care, disclose financial incentives and provide continuity of care. An internal and external appeals process for consumers who have grievances with health providers or plans has been developed. And, FEHBP plans are prohibited from imposing gag rules on participating physicians.

NARFE also endorsed the strong and enforceable patient protections in S. 1052, "Bipartisan Patients' Protection Act", as approved by the Senate on June 29, 2001. In addition, we specifically supported S. 1052's FEHBP liability provisions -- as included in Senator Don Nickles' amendment to the bill -- because federal employees and annuitants should receive the same accountable and enforceable protections that other Americans will acquire through the Patients' Bill of Rights and because new costs are likely to be nominal.

We also support significant improvements in mental health and substance abuse parity in FEHBP plans that were made in response to the 1999 White House Conference on Mental Health recommendations.

Senator Pete Domenici told the Senate Health, Education, Labor and Pensions (HELP) Committee in July 2001 that breathtaking medical advances have occurred because health insurance has covered ailments like heart disease while "those suffering from a mental illness do not enjoy those same benefits of treatment and medical advances because all too often insurance discriminates against illnesses of the brain." As Senator Domenici said to the HELP Committee, the cost of mental health parity "is negligible, especially contrasted with the cost impact to society." NARFE supports continuation of mental health and substance abuse parity in FEHBP.

Shifting Costs to Enrollees

Proposals to shift costs to enrollees -- that are cynically promoted as cost containment or consumer choice initiatives – have been suggested by some during previous rate hikes.

For example, in the fiscal year (FY) 1999 Budget Resolution, the House Budget Committee sought to limit annual growth in the government's share of FEHBP premiums to the consumer price index (CPI). According to a Congressional Budget Office (CBO) estimate prepared in 1997, the federal government would have cost-shifted $400 in added annual cost to federal annuitants and employees in 2002 and more in later years if this artificial limitation had become law. The entirety of federal government budget savings would have been attributed to shifting costs to enrollees. Indeed, federal employees and annuitants would have paid an ever-increasing proportion of premium costs each year FEHBP rate hikes exceeded general inflation as measured by the CPI. This was a virtual guarantee, given the historical pattern where premium increases have outpaced inflation.

Other proposals have been made to offer a cafeteria-style benefit offering to federal workers and annuitants. Under this approach, federal employees -- and perhaps annuitants -- would receive a tax–free fixed dollar government/employer contribution, adjusted annually for inflation, to pay for FEHBP, life insurance and presumably the Thrift Savings Plan. Like the premium-indexing proposal included in the FY 1999 budget resolution, this proposal would limit future government contributions to the CPI and costs above general inflation would be shifted to enrollees. The lump-sum government contribution could also force employees and annuitants to forgo one benefit to pay for another, and in the case of FEHBP, could increase the number of uninsured persons. While NARFE supports informing consumers and incentives to control health costs, we oppose forcing only enrollees to shoulder the burden of increased premiums.

NARFE also is concerned about any proposal that would end the present limit on the FEHBP government contribution to 75 percent. Such an initiative has been included in the FEHBPinspired "premium support" Medicare reform plan. Under FEHBP, enrollees pay at least 25 percent of their health plan premiums. Absent this cap, the enrollee share of FEHBP premiums could be zero if enrollees select the lowest cost plans -- giving enrollees a "premium-free" option. This option could have a significant effect on the rest of the program. The availability of a no-cost plan would serve as a particularly strong incentive to younger, healthier employees. Unintended risk selection occurs when enrollees leave plans where risk is more likely to be widespread, and leads more enrollees to congregate in the no-cost plans. Since the FEHBP "Fair Share" government contribution formula is weighted to the number of enrollees, no-cost plans that attract large shares of enrollees would reduce the overall dollar amount of the maximum government contribution under the premium support proposal. Consequently, costs would be shifted to enrollees in all other plans, increasing enrollee costs and effectively limiting consumer choice.

A plan included in the Administration's FY 2003 budget to formally coordinate Medicare and FEHBP coverage by "offer[ing] insurance plans tailored to the federal retiree..." is another proposal that could shift costs to enrollees – specifically annuitants. As you know, there is presently no difference between the FEHBP plans offered to federal employees, annuitants and Medicare-participating annuitants.

Although there is coordination of coverage between traditional Medicare and FEHBP fee-for-service plans, less synchronization of benefits exists between managed care plans and Medicare. NARFE expressed concerns last year that a separately- rated FEHBP health plan for Medicare-participating retirees and survivors might be suggested in response to the Administration's budget proposal.

One of the chief advantages of a large, employer-sponsored group health insurance program, like the FEHBP, is that the risk of health costs are spread across a diverse community. Segregating retirees from that community would destroy such risk sharing and significantly increase premiums. We also concerned that coverage under a separate annuitant health plan would be inferior to benefits currently available to all FEHBP enrollees.

Shifting benefit costs to individuals devoting, or who have devoted, their careers to public service is the wrong signal to send at any time, particularly when the federal government is facing a human capital crisis. Moreover, premium indexing, premium support, separate annuitant health plan and some cafeteria-style benefit proposals do nothing to contain costs. We urge the subcommittee to oppose these and other proposals to shift costs to federal employees and annuitants.

Medical Savings Accounts and Other "Customer-Driven" Schemes

NARFE is also disturbed by the American Postal Workers Union (APWU) and the OPM's decision to offer a so-called "customer-driven" option in FEHBP for 2003 because they are significantly similar to costly Medical Savings Accounts (MSAs).

MSAs are plans that combine a high deductible catastrophic insurance policy with a tax-exempt savings account dedicated for health care expenses. Although the "Personal Care Account" (PCA) component of the APWU customer-driven plan is not tax-exempt, and provides "credits" toward health care instead of cash, its purpose and function are comparable to the savings account portion of an MSA.

MSAs and other "customer driven" financing schemes can be attractive to healthier enrollees since the plans reward them with either cash balances or extra coverage in subsequent years if they don't go to the doctor or to a hospital. As a result, healthy individuals are siphoned into the new option and premiums in the comprehensive plans they left must be increased in response (known as "adverse selection"). Consequently, MSAs and related plans could circumvent the fundamental principles of group health insurance by dividing healthy and sick persons into different coverage options. The Congressional Budget Office (CBO) says that legislation to make MSAs available in FEHBP would cost taxpayers nearly $1 billion over five years.

Providing cash or credit balances at the end of the year to anyone who believes their health care costs will be low is a powerful incentive for enrollment. However, this incentive also could encourage FEHBP enrollees to "game" the system by switching to a comprehensive plan during the program's annual "open season" in any year they know their health care expenses will multiply. This "gaming" only will exacerbate the adverse selection anticipated from the introduction of MSAs or "customer-driven" plans in FEHBP.

During the OPM's September 18 press conference, agency officials repeatedly said that the new APWU plan was not an MSA. In response to a question on whether the new option would cause adverse selection in existing comprehensive options, OPM benefit specialists said it would not happen because the APWU plan does not operate like an MSA. However, when asked how the new plan would coordinate with Medicare for annuitants, officials said that the APWU plan would not be attractive to most retirees. For instance, unlike most FEHBP fee-for-service plans used with Medicare, the "customer driven" scheme would not waive deductibles, coinsurance and copayments. Later in the press conference, OPM staff recognized that the new plan created the "potential for adverse selection" and asserted that they would monitor possible risk selection. Because the APWU plan sets a new precedence in FEHBP, we are troubled that current and future "customer driven" options will continued to be offered in the program regardless of their harmful effects on the federal community's risk pool.

Finally, we strongly object to OPM's decision to withhold information about the APWU plan until the September 18 press conference. As a result, there was no opportunity to publicly review the plan by FEHBP stakeholders – like NARFE and other federal community organizations – or by Congress before the lateness of the contracting process made changing or withdrawing the plan improbable. OPM's handling of the APWU introduction stands in stark contrast to their announcement of the Blue Cross/Blue Shield "basic option" plan in 2001 when interested parties and Congress were made aware of the new plan several months before contracts with insurance carriers were finalized.

During NARFE's two most recent biennial national conventions, delegates considered several resolutions to support legislation that would give our association a formal or advisory role in OPM's FEHBP contract negotiations with carriers. Our delegates were persuaded not to adopt this policy because the informal relationship between OPM and NARFE was adequate in previous negotiations to represent our interests. This argument cannot be made in the future if the APWU introduction this year is used as a model and there are no opportunities for stakeholders to review new FEHBP options in advance.

We are hopeful that future announcements do not include using new "health reimbursement accounts" (HRAs) with high deductible catastrophic health insurance as a proxy to offering MSAs in FEHBP. Likewise, while we support making Flexible Savings Accounts (FSAs) available to federal annuitants, we are concerned that they also could be used as an MSA substitute if legislation is enacted to allow FSA balances to be rolled over from year-to-year.

Although MSAs, "customer driven" and related plans may provide short-term financial gains to some enrollees, their growth in FEHBP could result in higher costs for enrollees and taxpayer in the long run. It is simply a mistake to transform a successful group health system -- where risk sharing keeps health insurance affordable and predictable throughout life -- to an "every man for himself" scheme – where premiums and out-of-pocket expenses are only reasonable for healthy participants.

Conclusion

For 41 years the FEHBP has minimized costs and provided a wide choice of comprehensive health insurance plans to nearly nine million federal employees, retirees and their families. OPM's ability to minimize expenses is now being challenged by significantly higher health care costs. I can assure this committee, that adequate, affordable health care coverage is of paramount importance to retirees. NARFE stands ready to work with this panel, others in Congress and the OPM to find ways and means of containing out-of-control health care costs without sacrificing quality, access and coverage without resorting to proposals that only shift costs to enrollees or that circumvent risk sharing in our group plan environment.

Mr. WELDON. We will now hear from Mr. Bobby Harnage. You are recognized for 5 minutes, sir.

Mr. HARNAGE. Thank you, Mr. Chairman and Congressman Davis. On behalf of the more than 600,000 Federal and D.C. government employees our union represents, I thank you for the opportunity to testify today on the problems plaguing the Federal Employee Health Benefit Program.

Because of the ability of the insurance companies to use their financial and political power to influence the decisions of the Office of Personnel Management, both taxpayers and Federal employees, including retirees, pay far too much for the benefits they receive under the program. In addition, the formula for determining Federal employees financial burden for the program is too low. It undermines the competitiveness of the entire Federal compensation package and contributes to the government's ongoing problems in recruitment and retaining the next generation of Federal employees.

The program, which covers almost 9 million active and retired Federal employees and their dependents, is the Nation's largest employer-sponsored health insurance plan. Although politicians in recent years have touted FEHBP as a model health care plan, its participants consider it anything but a model, primarily because of rapidly increasing premium costs.

In 2003, the average premiums will rise by 11.2 percent. This increase follows the pattern of the last 5 years, so that over the past 6 years the average premium increased by 61 percent. These sorts of premiums have far outpaced Federal pay increases, the cost of the living measured by the CPI, and importantly, the rate of increase in health care spending nationally.

Those who don't participate are also adversely affected by these premium hikes. There are 250,000 Federal employees who are eligible to participate in the program, but remain uninsured; and the reason commonly cited by them is the cost. The terms offered to Federal employees under the program are substantially worse than those offered to employees of other large unionized employers both in the public and private sector.

While the Federal Government pays just 72 percent of the weighted average premium, but not more than 75 percent, large employers in the private sector and several large States pay at least 80 percent and often 100 percent of the premiums according to the recent data published by the Bureau of Labor Statistics and the Kaiser Family Foundation.

Employees of the U.S. Postal Service bargain collectively over their employer's share of the cost. The Postal Service pays 85 percent of the premium, while postal workers pay only 15 percent. The FDIC, a Federal agency that regulates the banking industry, also negotiates with their employees over health insurance and pays 85 percent on the premium as well. In both cases, the employer does so not because of the overwhelming power of the union but because it is a "best practices" business decision to do so.

The time has come for the Federal Government to improve its funding of the FEHBP and provide all Federal employees with a better premium split.

In the 107th Congress, Representative Steny Hoyer and Senator Barbara Mikulski have introduced legislation which would have changed the financing formula so that agencies pay approximately 80 percent on the premium. This legislation would have improved the affordability of the program immensely. Moving toward an average of 85 percent would have made the program more affordable for Federal workers and their families. It also would have been a smart response to the Federal Government's much discussed human capital crisis.

Closing the gap between the Federal Government and other employers in both the private-sector and public-sector area of insurance would have gone a long way toward improving the prospects of recruiting and retaining the next generation of Federal employees.

AFGE strongly opposes OPM's decision in September 2002 to grant carriers a permanent waiver from the cost accounting standards. We support the position taken by the full House in July 2002, when it refused to extend the CAS waivers for the carriers. Considering the widespread and serious accounting scandals that have emerged in the past year, along with the extraordinary premium increases over the past several years, it is imperative that standards be placed to make sure that the government insurance carriers are prevented from passing on illegitimate overhead costs to enrollees and taxpayers, which has happened repeatedly in the past. The use of CAS would simply ensure uniformity and consistency in the measurement, assignment and allocation of the cost of the Federal Government's contract with the carriers.

Indeed, the corporate accounting scandals that have so shaken the American peoples' confidence in the Nation's financial sector are the direct result of allowing firms to make up their accounting rules as they go along. The CAS are already used successfully by the agencies responsible for the administration of TRICARE and Medicare. In fact, many of the same carriers who participate in those programs comply with CAS are also FEHBP contractors.

There is only one particular carrier that is opposing the use of CAS, Blue Cross/Blue Shield. Other carriers, Federal employee unions and the OMB support using CAS to ensure that all carriers submit honest bills. Only Blue Cross stands in the way.

Blue Cross trotted out arguments in defense of its position: FEHBP is not a large part of its business, but that is precisely why the CAS are so necessary. Carriers bill the Federal Government for the costs they incur. However, absent the application of CAS, administrations have no idea what methods the carriers use to calculate those costs and whether the carriers' bills are reliable. The CAS prevents carriers from passing on to enrollees and taxpayers costs incurred by the carriers from their non-FEHBP contractors.

Blue Cross/Blue Shield spokesmen also insist that it is too expensive for the carrier to use CAS, but the cost of applying CAS is an allowable cost that will be charged to the program. In other words, ending the sort of accounting chicanery practiced so ruinously by Enron and other firms would not cost Blue Cross/Blue Shield a dime. And as has been the case with defense contracting, university research contracting, Medicare, TRICARE, and any cost-based reimbursement contract, the application of the CAS standards would be a modest investment that would yield significant dividends for taxpayers and enrollees.

Mr. Chairman, I look forward to working with you and this committee and other lawmakers within the Congress to help reduce the cost to the taxpayers and the participants to this program. I am sure it can be done if we make up our minds to do so.

This concludes my statement. I thank you for the opportunity to appear before the committee. I will be happy to answer any questions the members of the committee may have.

Mr. WELDON. Thank you very much for your testimony.

[The prepared statement of Mr. Harnage follows:]

INTRODUCTION

My name is Bobby L. Harnage and I am the National President of the American Federation of Government Employees, AFL-CIO (AFGE). On behalf of the more than 600,000 federal and District of Columbia employees our union represents, I thank you for the opportunity to testify today on the numerous problems plaguing the Federal Employees Health Benefits Program (FEHBP).

Because of its poor structure and the ability of its participating insurance carriers to use their financial and political power to manipulate the Office of Personnel Management's (OPM) administrative decisions, both taxpayers and federal employees and retirees pay far too much for the benefits they receive under the program. In addition, the formula for determining federal employees' financial burden for FEHBP undermines the competitiveness of the entire federal compensation package, and contributes to the government's ongoing problems in recruiting and retaining the next generation of federal employees.

FEHBP 2003 PREMIUM INCREASES

The Federal Employees Health Benefits Program, which currently covers almost nine million active and retired federal employees and their dependents, is the nation's largest employer-sponsored health insurance plan. Although politicians in recent years have touted FEHBP as a model health insurance plan, its participants consider it anything but a model – primarily because of rapidly increasing premium costs.

In 2003, average FEHBP premiums will rise by 11.2%. This increase follows the general pattern of 1998, 1999, 2000, 2001, and 2002 when the Office of Personnel Management approved average hikes of 7.2%, 9.5%, 9.3%, 10.5%, and 13.3% respectively. Over the past six years (1998-2003), the average premium increased by 61%. These soaring FEHBP premiums outpaced federal pay increases (generally around 3% to 4%), the cost-of-living measured by the Consumer Price Index (hovering around 2% to 3%), and the rate of increase in health care spending nationally (rising 6% to 7% annually).

The FEHBP nonparticipants are also adversely impacted by the rapidly increasing FEHBP premiums. Of the 250,000 federal employees who are eligible to participate in FEHBP but remain uninsured, the reason most commonly cited by them to explain their lack of participation is its prohibitive cost. As a result, the FEHBP does not succeed in the most basic test of a health insurance program: it does not produce universal coverage for its target population – federal employees, retirees, and their families.

FEHBP's premium costs are shared by the federal government and the participating employee. But the terms offered to federal employees under FEHBP are substantially worse than those offered to the employees of other large, unionized employers, both in the private and public sectors. While the federal government pays according to a formula that covers just 72% of the weighted average premium, but not more than 75%; large employers in the private sector and several large states pay at least 80% and often 100% of premiums, according to recent data published by the Bureau of Labor Statistics and the Kaiser Family Foundation.

Within the federal government itself, employees of the U.S. Postal Service bargain collectively over both wages and their employer's share of FEHBP health insurance benefits. The Postal Service pays 85% of FEHBP premiums while postal workers pay only 15%. The Federal Deposit Insurance Corporation (FDIC), a federal agency that regulates the banking industry, also negotiates with its employees over health insurance and pays 85% of FEHBP premiums as well. In both cases, the employer does so not because of the overwhelming power of the union, but because it is a "best practices" business decision to do so.

The time has come for the federal government to improve its funding of FEHBP, and provide federal employees with a better premium split.

In the 107th Congress, Rep. Steny Hoyer (D-MD) and Senator Barbara Mikulski (D-MD) introduced legislation (H.R. 1307 and S. 1982) which would have changed the financing formula for FEHBP so that agencies would pay approximately 80 percent of the premiums for federal employees who have

FEHBP health care coverage. This legislation would have improved the affordability of FEHBP immensely. Moving to an average of 80% would have made FEHBP more affordable for federal workers and their families. It would have opened the door to health insurance to many of the 250,000 uninsured federal workers who cannot afford coverage at today's rates. It also would have been a smart response to the federal government's much discussed "human capital crisis." Closing the gap between the federal government and other employers in both the private and public sectors in the area of health insurance benefits would have gone a long way toward improving prospects for recruiting and retaining the next generation of federal employees.

COST ACCOUNTING STANDARDS

AFGE strongly opposes OPM's decision in September 2002 to grant FEHBP carriers a permanent waiver from the Cost Accounting Standards (CAS). Instead, we support the position taken by the full House in July 2002 when it refused to extend for yet another year the CAS waiver for FEHBP carriers. During its consideration of the FY 2003 Treasury-Postal Service appropriations bill (H.R. 5120), the House approved **by voice vote** an amendment offered by Rep. Dennis Kucinich (D-OH) to strike the bill's section that exempted FEHBP carriers from CAS.

Considering the widespread and serious accounting scandals that have emerged in the past year, along with the extraordinary FEHBP premium increases over the last several years, it is imperative that standards be in place to make sure that the government's insurance carriers are prevented from passing on illegitimate overhead costs to enrollees and taxpayers, as has happened repeatedly in the past. The use of CAS would simply ensure uniformity and consistency in the measurement, assignment, and allocation of the costs of the federal government's contracts with FEHBP carriers. Indeed, the corporate accounting scandals that have so shaken the American people's confidence in the nation's financial sector are the direct result of allowing firms to make up the accounting rules as they go along. The CAS are already used successfully by the agencies responsible for the administration of TRICARE and Medicare. In fact, many of the same carriers who participate in those programs and comply with CAS are also FEHBP contractors.

There is only one particular FEHBP carrier that is opposing the use of CAS: Blue Cross/Blue Shield. Other FEHBP carriers, federal employee unions, and OMB support using CAS to ensure that all carriers submit honest bills. Only Blue Cross/Blue Shield stands in the way.

Blue Cross/Clue Shield has half-heartedly trotted out arguments in defense of its position. FEHBP is not a large part of its business, the carrier's spokespersons insist. But that is precisely why the CAS are so necessary. FEHBP carriers bill the federal government for the costs they incur. However, absent the application of the CAS, FEHBP administrators have no idea what methods the carriers use to calculate those costs and whether the carriers' bills are reliable. The CAS prevent carriers from passing on to enrollees and taxpayers costs incurred by the carriers from their non-FEHBP contracts. The more non-FEHBP business a carrier has, the more incentive that carrier has to pass on costs incurred in the cost of that non-FEHBP business to the taxpayers and enrollees who pay FEHBP premiums.

Blue Cross/Blue Shield spokespersons also insist that it is too expensive for the carrier to use the CAS. But the cost of applying CAS is an allowable cost that would be charged to the program. In other words, ending the sort of accounting chicanery practiced so ruinously by Enron and other firms would not cost Blue Cross/Blue Shield a dime. And as has been the case with defense contracting, university research contracting, Medicare, TRICARE, and any cost-based reimbursement contract, the application of the CAS standards would be a modest investment that would yield significant dividends for the taxpayers and enrollees who pay for FEHBP in terms of increased accountability and reduced premiums.

PERSONAL CARE ACCOUNTS

AFGE opposes the introduction of the highly destructive Personal Care Accounts (PCAs), the Medical Savings Account-type of health plans, that the Office of Personnel Management decided in September 2002 to offer the nine million participants in the Federal Employees Health Benefits Program (FEHBP) through the American Postal Workers Union (APWU) Health Plan. It is worth noting that OPM failed to provide any consultation or pre-notification that it was considering the introduction of this radical change into FEHBP. AFGE and other organizations that represent those who are forced to foot the bill for OPM's allegiance to the insurance companies' interests were presented with what they call their "doughnut" plan as a *fait accompli*.

This action typifies OPM's approach to administering FEHBP: It views the insurance companies as its "partners" while Congress, federal agencies, federal employees and retirees, those who pay the bills, are viewed as irrelevant. In the case of these pre-Medical Savings Accounts, the partner in question is a corporate entity to create a market for medical savings account-types of plan. The Definity Health Corporation that stands behind the introduction of PCAs joins Merrill Lynch, Kohlberg Kravis Roberts and other big financiers with Merck Medco, PriceWaterhouseCoopers, Active Health Management and others represents a formidable political and economic powerhouse.

The PCAs that OPM has worked out in partnership with Definity Corporation work as follows: The federal government puts pre-tax money ($1,000 for a single person, $2,000 for families) into a special PCA, and employees use that money to pay for their medical expenses. Any money left in the employees' PCA at year-end rolls over for use by employees for future medical expenses. If employees' annual medical costs exceed the money in their PCA, they are responsible for their own medical expenses, up to $600 for single people and $1,200 for families. After employees have used up both their PCA and deductible, the federal government begins paying 85% of their medical expenses.

The basic problem with PCAs – as with the more traditional MSAs – is that they will worsen the "risk segmentation" in the FEHBP market, resulting in increases in the premiums of conventional, low-deductible health insurance that have nothing to do with either increased utilization or improved benefits.

Risk segmentation takes place when young/healthy and older/less healthy segments of the population become segregated into different types of insurance plans. With the introduction of PCAs, FEHBP's problems with risk segmentation will become worse because substantial numbers of young, healthy people with low medical costs will choose to use PCAs. This will leave people who are older, less healthy – and have higher medical costs – in conventional, low-deductible health insurance plans, and cause their premiums to rise by more than they otherwise would.

These divisions in the FEHBP market drive up the cost of conventional, low-deductible insurance for the older, less healthy segments of the population who are least likely to afford the premiums. Insurance markets are based on the principle of cross-subsidy, reflecting average risk of a diverse risk pool. When healthier people choose PCAs, the risk characteristics of the pool that remains in conventional health insurance plans will rise by more than they would without PCAs. The plans offering conventional insurance will incur higher-than-average medical costs because healthier people will no longer be in the pool, and premiums for conventional insurance will rise.

OPM will report the "cause" of these increases in premiums as an increase in utilization and the cost of technology. But that type of "analysis" will be obfuscation. When those who utilize medical care and medical technology are forced to congregate in the remaining FEHBP plans which still allow comprehensive coverage, the cost of insurance for them rises. The prices charged to them will not reflect the actuarial value of the benefits provided but rather, the risk characteristics of the group. Thus, those most likely to use medical care will pay the highest prices for that care. If there were less risk segmentation, the utilization of medical care by the FEHBP population would be the same, yet taxpayers and enrollees would pay less for that care because it would be covered under premiums that reflected a lower average risk.

Thus the inflation that OPM reports as causing inflation is just a reflection of the structural flaws OPM has helped engineer into FEHBP. And the introduction of the new "consumer driven" plan will only exacerbate those flaws.

CONCLUSION

This concludes my statement. I will be happy to answer any questions the members of the Committee may have.

Mr. WELDON. We will now conclude with Mr. Scandlen.

You are recognized for 5 minutes.

Mr. SCANDLEN. Thank you, Mr. Chairman. I am fighting a cold, so please indulge me.

I appreciate the opportunity to come here. I am not actually an expert in FEHBP. All of my work has been in the private sector with business organizations, insurance companies and the new innovations that are happening out in the world. I know that the private sector certainly learns a lot of lessons from FEHBP, and they watch it very closely. And my friends at the Heritage Foundation, for instance, are touting FEHBP as a model that the private sector should follow.

At the same time, I think it is worthwhile for the FEHBP to be looking at what's happening in the private sector and possibly learn from that as well. Education tends to be a two-way street.

The most interesting thing that's happening out in the world these days is a decisive move my employers toward consumer-driven health care. In part this is due to the disappointing track record of managed care and the backlash that employees have had toward managed care and the restrictions that have been placed on that. But it is also interesting that it is sparked by the medical savings account law that Congress passed in 1996. That law had many, many flaws and weaknesses, and the products coming out of that law have not been a huge success. However, one of the consequences of it is to force people, H.R. executives, insurance companies, benefit consultants, all sorts of people, to rethink the way consumers relate to health benefits. And for the first time ever, I think people are beginning to wonder whether consumers are able to control more of their own resources, make more of their own decisions.

Certainly we see that consumers did not care for having insurance company executives make major medical decisions for them. That is the underlying cause of the managed care backlash. If we are not doing that, what are we going to do? And, increasingly, I think people are coming to the conclusion that many health care decisions could be made by the consumer him- or herself if he has control of the resources, which means money.

The IRS issued a decision in June creating what the service calls a "health reimbursement arrangement." It's profoundly important. I argue it is every bit as important as the exclusion that the IRS issued 50 years ago, allowing employer-sponsored health insurance programs to be free of taxes for the employee. The HRA decision is similarly important, only it applies to cash accounts and puts cash accounts on an equal footing with the insurance products.

We do not yet know all the consequences of this, and there is a whole lot of thinking going on even as we speak on exactly what it means and exactly what the optimal product designs are going to be. One example is certainly the program that the postal workers have offered through FEHBP, and that is very interesting and a lot of companies are following that model. It's not the be-all and end-all of what could be done with this. However, some companies are looking at carving out prescription drug benefits for an HRA approach, so you have a deductible that applies to prescription drugs and cash accounts so people can pay directly up to some level. Others are increasing copayments or coinsurance rather than having an across the board deductible.

We are entering an era of just vast innovation and we don't yet know what the best balance is going to be between a cash account and an insurance product.

There are a lot of other things that the FEHBP could learn from the private sector also; how to preserve an indemnity option is certainly one of them. Very few insurance companies are actually licensed and active in 50 States. Some are active in all but two or three States; others prefer a regional approach; others may be a single-State approach. The requirement that a private indemnity carrier be available in all 50 States simply kills your indemnity option. There are very few companies that can comply with that.

And the same requirement obviously does not apply to HMOs. HMOs can be offered only in those areas where they're active. I would suggest that if you want to maintain a private indemnity option, that the same approach should be applied to HMOs.

There are a lot of other things. I think medical savings accounts are not just for the healthy and wealthy, and all the empirical evidence and all the research says just the opposite actually, that the wealthiest people prefer HMO coverage and the healthiest people prefer no coverage at all. Medical savings accounts are good for everybody, and if that is the case, I would love to continue meeting with you in the future.

Thank you.

Mr. WELDON. Well, thank you, Mr. Scandlen.

[The prepared statement of Mr. Scandlen follows:]

Statement of Greg Scandlen

to the

Subcommittee on Civil Service, Census, and Agency Organization

of the

Committee on Government Reform

of the

United States House of Representatives

December 11, 2002

Mr. Chairman and Members of the Committee,

Thank you for the opportunity to share some thoughts with you on the health benefits program for federal employees.

I am Greg Scandlen, currently working with the Galen Institute as a consulting Fellow in Health Policy. I have been involved in health care policy and health care financing for twenty-four years.

As you know, the FEHBP is widely considered a success story, and this Committee should be congratulated for its oversight of this important program. For many years, the FEHBP has provided some 9 million people with a range of first-rate coverage at affordable prices and a minimum of bureaucratic meddling. Even today with health care costs rising dramatically, the FEHBP has managed to restrain those increases. I note that FEHBP premiums are rising some eleven percent this year, while the similar program in California, CalPERS, is experiencing increases of double that amount and reducing the options available to CalPERS enrollees.

The private sector pays attention to the successes you have had and learns from your experience. Certainly my friends at the Heritage Foundation have trumpeted FEHBP as a model for reforming health care throughout the nation.

At the same time, there is much the FEHBP could learn from the private sector as well. One of the marvels of our economic and political system is our ability to constantly experiment, innovate, learn, and grow. Even if we could identify a perfect program or a perfect product today, it would need to be changed in two or three years to keep up with changes in the economy, technology, health care trends, and the demographics and preferences of the evolving workforce.

So, I congratulate you on continuing to look at how the program can be improved for the good of not only federal workers but also the taxpayers who fund these benefits.

WHAT FEHBP CAN LEARN FROM THE PRIVATE SECTOR

With that, let me share with you some insights about the changes that are taking place in the private sector and how those changes might be incorporated into FEHBP.

Certainly the biggest change is the new and growing movement towards "consumer-driven" and "defined contribution" health care. Consumer-driven health care is based on several ideas:

1. For most routine health care encounters, consumers are able, willing, and eager to make their own decisions and their own judgments about what is right for them.
2. Relying on third-parties to make these decisions is wasteful, inefficient, and unsatisfactory to the people who count – the patients.
3. In order to make rational decisions, consumers need two things that have been unavailable in the past -- information and control over resources.
4. Part of the reason reliable information has not been available in the past is because without control of resources consumers did not demand the information. There was little they could do with the information, even if it were available.

What is true with health care encounters is even more true in selecting health care plans. As FEHBP has demonstrated, we have a diverse and mobile workforce. Different people have different needs. Some people like the one-stop shopping aspect of a staff model HMO, and are willing to surrender some choice to get it. Other people feel just the opposite. They don't care for the constraints HMOs put on their choice of doctor or hospital, and they want the freedom to choose from any licensed provider. Each person should be able to choose the health plan that best suits his or her needs. And this is the essential idea behind defined contribution health care.

When you put the two concepts together you have a very powerful notion that will revolutionize health care. They both rely on a well-informed consumer making decisions about their own health care needs and values. But consumers will not be able to make these value judgments without also knowing the cost consequences of their decisions. They need to control their own resources, as well as simply having choices.

EMPOWERING CONSUMERS

In 1996, Congress enacted legislation allowing the creation of Medical Savings Accounts. For all the flaws of that legislation, it has had a huge impact on the way people think about health care financing. Decision makers – employers, insurers, benefits consultants, human resource executives – all were forced to think anew about the role of consumers in health care. Can people really do this? Can they make their own decisions, or do all decisions need to be made by sharp-penciled insurance executives?

The question has been answered empirically by the experience with managed care. While some people love managed care, many, many others do not. They particularly do not like the whole idea of insurance executives making health care decisions for them. They have insisted on making their own choices.

Given that stark reality, employers have begun to look for ways to empower consumers, and they have had the lesson of Medical Savings Accounts to draw from. They are not eligible to make use of Archer MSAs, but they have found ways to replicate the MSA design within current law and their own benefits programs.

HEALTH REIMBURSEMENT ARRANGEMENTS

In June of this year, the Internal Revenue Service gave this movement an enormous boost by issuing a Notice and Revenue Ruling allowing the creation of what the Service termed "Health Reimbursement Arrangements" (HRAs).

This decision will impact the benefits market as profoundly as the IRS decision fifty years ago that employer-sponsored health plans would be excluded from the income of employees. That decision also was prompted by what employers were already doing, and the need to clarify the tax status of this new trend. It was later codified by Congress, much as HRAs will likely be in the next few years.

But the decision fifty years ago applied only to health insurance programs sponsored by employers. This new ruling applies to cash accounts sponsored by employers. The Service has placed cash accounts on an equal footing with insurance programs.

FLEXIBILITY AND EXPERIMENTATION

And as with the exclusion of fifty years ago, this new ruling allows complete flexibility. The only restrictions are that the accounts may be funded solely by the employer, and the funds may be spent solely on health care services as defined in Section 213(d) of the Code. Other than that, the accounts may be of any amount of money, they may accompany any kind of insurance plan or none at all, they may be funded or unfunded, they may be rolled over and collect interest from year to year, and they may be accessed even post-employment to help pay for COBRA premiums, retiree benefits, or direct payment of health care services.

The consequences are profound. We don't yet know what the optimal use of these funds will be. Most immediately, employers are setting up programs similar to what the Postal Workers are offering under FEHBP. This includes a high deductible for most services, first dollar coverage of certain preventive and wellness services, a cash account to fill in the gaps, and extensive information and decision support. Other employers might use an HRA to offset increased coinsurance or higher co-payments, or they might carve out prescription drug benefits and apply an HRA just to that. One vendor is offering a product that has a high deductible for what it calls discretionary services, but no deductible for non-discretionary services such as inpatient surgery and maintenance drugs for hypertension or cholesterol.

There will be a period of experimentation as the market searches for the optimal balance of cash accounts and insured benefits. I expect that in just a few years virtually every employer will be using some form of HRA to supplement its insured benefits programs. The FEHBP will want to monitor this development closely to see what direction the market takes. It may be that an arrangement like that of the Postal Workers is optimal, but it is equally likely that there will be variations on the theme that FEHBP will want to replicate.

DEFINED CONTRIBUTION

The private sector is also experimenting with defined contribution programs. These are similar to what FEHBP is already doing in that individual employees can choose the benefits program they prefer. But there are some important differences. Most of the programs are being offered by a single carrier, often a Blue Cross Blue Shield plan, which helps allay some of the selection concerns. The employer makes a fixed contribution to the cost of premium and the employee may buy a higher or lower benefits package depending on his or her own values. Employees pay their share of the premium on a tax-free basis through a Section 125 premium conversion plan.

Unlike FEHBP, which pays no more than 75% of the premium regardless of the plan chosen, these programs make a fixed dollar amount available and if there is a plan available that is fully paid by that contribution, the employee may not have to contribute to the premium at all. The FEHBP should consider this approach as a way of encouraging workers to choose lower cost options. Theoretically, an employee might choose a plan that costs less than the fixed contribution, in which case the excess contribution could be put into an HRA.

PRESERVING AN INDEMNITY OPTION

There are some other lessons for the FEHBP in the private sector as well. Certainly one is how to retain a private indemnity option. FEHBP currently requires that a private indemnity carrier be licensed in all fifty states to participate in the program. But the reality is that very few carriers, if any, are licensed or active in all fifty states. Most are regional, focusing on a particular geographic area. Some are licensed in every state but one or two because of the unique regulatory environment of those outlier states. Some carriers may even be active in only their home state, and have little interest in going elsewhere.

It defies logic that the FEHBP should disallow these carriers from participating in the program. HMOs are under no similar constraints. An HMO is perfectly free to define the geographic area it wishes to serve and offer benefits to federal employees only in those areas.

The fifty state indemnity requirement also advantages HMOs by allowing them to rate their premium solely on the health care costs that apply to that particular area, while an indemnity carrier has to offer the same premium to all federal workers across the country. Obviously health care costs are much lower in Kansas than they are in New York. An HMO based in Kansas can offer premiums that reflect the lower costs in that state, while an indemnity carrier has to average the costs in Kansas with the costs in New York. Kansans would be better off signing up for the local, less expensive HMO and avoiding the higher indemnity premiums. Just the opposite would be true for New Yorkers. So, even if a carrier were licensed in all fifty states, it would soon enough find that it was enrolling workers from only the most expensive geographic areas and would be uncompetitive and unprofitable.

COMMUNITY RATING

Consumer-driven health is forcing reconsideration of a lot of shibboleths. Community rating is one example. Community rating means everyone pays the same, regardless of age, geography, or health condition. But it also implies that employers with an HRA should contribute the same amount of dollars to each employee, regardless of age, geography or health status. Yet employers, especially self-insured employers, know perfectly well that they don't pay out in claims the same number of dollars for each employee. To the extent the HRA is simply swapping cash accounts for claims that would otherwise be paid by the employer, it doesn't make sense to give 25 year-old Sam the same contribution as 55 year-old Pete. Pete incurs a lot more claims than Sam and has a lot more expenses. If the company were paying the claims directly, it would be paying four times as much for Pete than for Sam. So, why not give Pete an HRA contribution of $1,000, while Sam gets an HRA contribution of $250?

Differential HRA contributions have not been adopted yet, but it is the kind of thing employers are mulling over, and FEHBP should, too. And the same principle applies to insurance premiums and defined contribution situations. It costs more to cover some people than others. It does not make sense to make the same contribution to everybody.

Even when it comes to the employee's share of premium, older workers place a higher value on their coverage than do younger workers, and they are willing to pay more for it. In fact, 56.1 percent of 50 year-old men have employer-based coverage in their own name, twice as many as 25 year-old men (28.6 percent), according to EBRI. Younger people are more likely to decline coverage because their share of the premium costs more than the coverage is worth to them. One way to keep younger people covered and included in the risk-pool, is to charge them a share of the premium that is actuarially fair. There are companies in the marketplace that do precisely this sort of premium reallocation.

CONCLUSION

We are entering an entirely new era for health benefits. Managed care will continue to be an important element, especially for high-cost, unusual conditions that are beyond the ability of most patients to manage. But most of the encounters we have with the health care system are routine and low-cost. This is not where most of the health care dollars are, but it is clearly where most of our personal experience is and where our perceptions of the health care system are formed.

To ensure greater satisfaction with health care, it is important that individual patients/workers/consumers have more control over these encounters than they have had in the past. It is within their ability to make these decisions once they have control over the resources and the information to make sensible judgments and trade-offs.

It is also far more efficient to enable patients to pay cash when they receive a service than it is to process claims through any sort of insurance mechanism. Such an arrangement should lower administrative costs both for insurers and for providers.

All of this is a dramatic departure from the way we have been doing things for the past fifty years. We are just now entering a period of rapid innovation and experimentation. Already some of the original business models have been revised, some of the ideas have been changed. Not every new idea will be a good one, and progress will depend on our ability to continue revising and perfecting the ideas in the light of market realities.

I will be happy to answer any questions you have.

Mr. WELDON. And I thank all of our witnesses. We certainly had a fair degree of diverse opinion, and hopefully we can explore some of these opinions more in the question-and-answer period.

Let me just recognize myself first for questions. And beginning with you, Mr. Francis, understanding that I have some experience in the arena that you are talking about where people would get a very good Medicare supplemental and then essentially throw all cost cautions to the wind—and indeed, I saw it on almost a daily basis when I practiced medicine—the issue that you brought up I thought was a very good one.

Understanding that we have always, every Congress, a very full plate and it is a very difficult process to get any piece of legislation through, which was—if you read the Federalist Papers, was the deliberate intent of the Founding Fathers—what would you say if we had to reform one thing within the FEHBP, or one or two things, what would you say are the highest priorities that you would suggest for us?

Mr. FRANCIS. I think one within your jurisdiction and one in the other committee, but I would submit to you, sir, I do not think there is any reason to think that the Ways and Means Committee believes that some important principle is being violated if the penalty on Medicare enrollment were not automatic for people in a situation like Federal retirees.

I also want to be clear, I am not saying people shouldn't be entitled to spend that $4,000 for Blue Cross and Medicare but let's give them a few other options so they are not forced to spend that exorbitant premium amount. I will call that my No. 2 priority.

The No. 1 is in your control. And I want to really just emphasize—let me use an analogy: If we had a program called car stamps, sort of like food stamps, the way we run the FEHBP, basically we say we will pay 75 percent of the cost of the car up to some very high number. If we offered a program like that for buying cars, maybe people wouldn't be buying Masaratis and Ferraris, but they would be buying very expensive SUVs and Cadillacs and Mercedes, because, after all, the government is paying three-fourths of the cost.

If, on the other hand, we had a program that said we will pay 100 percent of your car purchase up to the cost of a Honda Civic, I think we would see a whole lot more Honda Civics and nothing thereafter—a whole lot more Honda Civics bought.

OK, so the issue here is to provide much better first-dollar premium coverage benefiting low-wage Federal workers and retirees on a very strained budget, but at the same time employees and retirees have a greater cost exposure for their decision, if you will.

In other words, we can have our cake and eat it too, since you do have legislation introduced along the line of premium-sharing by the Federal Government, which could be very expensive.

I think the OPM estimate of over a billion is right for that particular bill. But, you know, you've got a session of Congress, you've got Members on both sides who are interested, and I think you have people around this table of every persuasion interested in seeing some improvements made that would both improve cost consciousness while improving the program for low-wage and low-earnings employees.

Mr. WELDON. Does anybody want to respond to what he just said, particularly from the unions? If not, then I will—Mrs. Kelly.

Mrs. KELLY. Overall the concept of providing, whether you call it a cafeteria plan, as you have, Mr. Chairman, or some base plan, anything that's ever been proposed in this arena in the past or has been discussed as a proposal talks about a flat amount of money, and that any increases in that would come through simple inflation. And one of the overriding concerns for NTEU is that in any discussions about that which we're willing to discuss anything to make the plan better, that our concern is that it would need to be tied to medical inflation, not to simple inflation, and if Congress were not willing to provide the resources to make that happen, then we don't see it as a viable plan after anything but a first-year try. So that is an overriding issue for us in our discussion about this.

Mr. WELDON. That's not an unreasonable position at all. One of the concerns, and I don't take this as a very serious concern, but nonetheless it's one of the things that comes to my mind, the issue of a number of Federal employees, it's been cited at 5 percent, who elect no insurance because of cost reasons I find very troubling, and certainly to go up to 100 percent of premium for a weighted average of whatever it would be, 75 percent, has anybody raised any concerns that if we did legislate that as an allowable option, that it would cause a stampede of beneficiaries to go to the lower benefit package? And maybe Mr. Scandlen, who's familiar with the private sector, can comment on this.

I don't personally think it would. I think consumers are much more savvy, and they understand the health benefits, but has that complaint been raised at all? Do any of you have that type of concern?

Mr. SCANDLEN. I think the private sector is going through very much a similar process. Many employers have in the past done a percentage of premium, and they are beginning to move away from that to a fixed contribution, as Walt suggested. We don't have empirical evidence yet about what the consequences are; however, I think there's also—employers are also increasing choices, and employers have been lagging behind the Federal—the Federal program in terms of the variety of choices. So I think one of the things that happens is increased choice at the same time they fix their contribution level, and I expect that employees are going to be a lot happier in that situation than they have been.

Mr. WELDON. I see my time has expired. I'm happy to recognize the gentleman from Illinois.

Mr. DAVIS OF ILLINOIS. Thank you very much, Mr. Chairman.

Mr. Francis, I was intrigued with your opening comments. Is it your position that copayments or copay might have more impact or influence on usage and ultimate costs than premiums?

Mr. FRANCIS. Yes, sir, I do believe that's the case. There's an immense amount of research out there on the influence of let's call it cost-sharing—it could be coinsurance, it could be deductibles, it could be copayments—on—on reducing health care costs. In fact, I used in my testimony a recent study by the Rand Corp. on prescription drug cost-sharing. They studied some methods used in the private sector that are very similar to those used in the FEHBP plans. That shouldn't be surprising because these plans evolve with the private sector, and it turns out that these several tier arrangements for prescription drugs have dramatic effects on how much people spend on prescription drugs, and they're not perverse effects. I mean, the—the issue is you want people to think twice whether they buy, for example, that $100-a-month Cox inhibitor for their arthritis or that $10-a-month one, and, you know, if they have to have the $100 one because of side effects, so be it, but—but they will be more frugal somewhere else.

Yeah. One could probably—I won't go through all the examples. Yes, huge effect from copayments from coinsurance, and that's why I'm so concerned about this 100 percent wraparound for people with Medicare because we're—we're not only making it more expensive for the program because they'll tend to overutilize, but we're also denying those people themselves the choice of having a greater mix of plans to let them sort of fine-tune their willingness to pay with their premium cost.

Mr. DAVIS OF ILLINOIS. Mr. Fallis, you were here and you've heard Mr. Francis' comments. How do you respond to those and the initial comments that he made that the FEHBP was in deep trouble? How do you respond to that from the vantage point of your membership?

Mr. FALLIS. Well, I listened to that, and that could very well be true, but my real concern is our members and our elderly retirees who have paid into this system since it began, and I'm typical of that. I began paying FEHBP premiums in 1960 when this program was—was instituted, and for 42 years I've paid premiums, and when I began, I was 33 years old, and I was young and healthy and robust, but I still paid that premium because I knew that someday I would be elderly and less healthy.

And I am opposed to any plan that we put into effect with FEHBP that will change the rules in the middle of the game after 42 years and leave elderly retirees hanging twisting in the wind. I know that if—if we use all kinds of changes here to siphon off the young and the healthy, and I've heard all the comments on this, but when you're left, when they leave one by one, we finally are left with a—with a risk pool of elderly, ill people, many, many hundreds, if not thousands and tens of thousands in my organization, who are going to be harmed by this. That's what we're concerned about; the premiums then, and what's left of this risk pool that we're in will double, triple, quadruple, or services will plummet to the point where the insurance policy will be practically worthless or, and I've heard nothing about this, the Congress will step up and recognize that these people should be held harmless, and they will make a decision to help them out with the premiums.

Mr. DAVIS OF ILLINOIS. So you're concerned that there would be enough balance so that there's not an adverse impact on your constituents; while overall something might be good for the whole system, but is adversely impacting those individuals that you have the most responsibility for?

Mr. FALLIS. That's exactly right. And there's something else going on here that hasn't been mentioned today. You know, we've talked about premium increases over the last 4 or 5 years being draconian, and I'm going to tell you those premium increases have hurt our people, but that's been the least of it. Since 1996, we've continually had the elderly on Medicare who year after year have seen—see their drug costs increase, the copays. They paid nothing until 1996, and then the system was changed.

You see, this is another foot in the door, getting the foot in the door and then—and then make changes. We now pay up to $35 for a 90-day supply of drugs, and this can be hundreds and thousands of dollars to some of our people and—and it's devastating, and so the premium increases are bad. You know, they're terrific, terrible, but that's in many cases the least of it.

Mr. DAVIS OF ILLINOIS. Thank you, Mr. Chairman.

Mrs. KELLY. Mr. Chairman, if I could just add——

Mr. WELDON. Sure.

Mrs. KELLY [continuing]. For just a short comment, I would echo Mr. Fallis's comments from this respect for NTEU. NTEU does not support there being two pools and the separation of current young, healthy, however you want to define, with retirees. I represent retired Federal workers as a part of NTEU, but probably more importantly my constituents today will be Mr. Fallis' constituents tomorrow because every Federal employee hopes to be a Federal retiree some day.

So I think—I think there are an awful lot of us that are—you know, that come at this from the same direction even though we might have different ideas or questions about how to get to a solution. But NTEU does not support creating separate pools in any way, shape, or form, however it's defined.

Mr. HARNAGE. If I might add to that, too, I—I support what he says 100 percent, but I feel like we're—we're trying to look at a defined contribution, whether a defined benefit, and we're looking at them especially with retirees as if it's a welfare program. Let's keep in mind these are earned benefits. This gentleman is talking about 42 years of service with the Federal Government and having difficulty in providing him and his family with continued health care in those years that he most needs it. This is not a welfare program. This is an earned program, and it should be a defined benefit, not a defined contribution.

Mr. WELDON. Let me just assure you, Mr. Fallis, at least as long as I'm around, I would never allow our retired Federal employees to twist in the wind when it comes to their health benefits.

I'm very pleased to recognize we've been joined by the gentlelady from the District of Columbia. You're recognized for questions.

Ms. NORTON. Thank you very much, Mr. Chairman. I appreciate that—that you're holding this hearing. You have even come in to have it.

I do want to say my regrets that I could not hear all the testimony. Believe it or not, this is not the only hearing being held today. I don't know what you call it, Mr. Chairman, a session after the lame duck session, but apparently that's what we're having now. But if ever an issue was worth it, certainly the FEHBP issue is worth it.

I won't ask questions relating to the testimony. One reason I wanted to come to this hearing is that I wanted to make sure that the notion that we tout all over the place, that the FEHBP system is a model for the country, continues to be true if it ever was true.

The testimony of Mr. Blair puzzles me somewhat because according to his testimony, we should be grateful for small favors; that is to say, there is a lower increase this year than there was last year. And I'm particularly interested in whether the FEHBP can go through another period as it did some years ago when it really had a reduction in the cost to employees. And I can't understand the difference—I no longer understand the difference between FEHBP and everybody else. So I no longer say, hey, aren't we lucky.

I want you to convince me that we are lucky. I know, and thanks to Mr. Blair's testimony, he says CALPERS is the second largest purchaser in the country. Am I to assume that the Federal Government is the first, largest employer purchaser in the country? They announced a rate up to 25 percent, up to 25 percent. See, I don't know what that means. I don't know what it means that the average person in that—got the same as FEHBP, but it got up to 25 percent. I mean, I don't know what that meant. I was beginning to think that the most important thing that FEHBP gave us was not economies of scale, which is what I always thought, but some convenience. I mean, somebody just put a bunch of things before us, and it's more convenient than going out into the marketplace.

I want you to make me understand why FEHBP is still the—what FEHBP provides that would not be the case if we were a part of some other system. Is it convenience? Do the economies of scale matter? I mean, if you are really twice—if really the second largest purchaser is more than twice as much, then maybe there is something to economies of scale.

How large is the second largest? That also doesn't tell me anything. I mean, I don't know whether to credit that or not. It's up to 25 percent. It's the second largest. It can be 1/10 as large as the Federal Government. So I really need some more information as I try to evaluate how good or not good FEHBP is. So if any of you can help me out, I'd appreciate it.

Mr. WELDON. Go ahead, Mr. Francis.

Mr. FRANCIS. I'll be glad to.

CALPERS is the California State employees system. It's pretty big. It's got—I forget—several, 3 million, something like that. I mean, we have 9 million. It's—that's not small potatoes. I think a large part of their problems unique to California, the—the managed care, crashing has been particularly severe there, and so some of it is just idiosyncratic to their circumstance. Also, they've been very successful holding down premiums over a lot of years, and so there's some catchup going on.

Having said that, I'd—I'd take a stand—by the way, the 25 percent increase is close to the average. They're seeing overall some plans much more than 25 percent.

Ms. NORTON. But that's peculiar to California.

Mr. FRANCIS. Well, it is and it isn't. The Mercer report just released, I don't know if OPM is quoting that one or not, but in the year 2002 the average employer health insurance—sponsored health insurance premium went up about 15 percent. So this program is outperforming, I think, still the private sector.

Just a partial answer to your other question, what drives this program, what makes it work is not per se the scale of it, it's the competition among plans to attract consumers. It's really a combination of keeping premiums down, keeping coinsurance down, and those two contradict, I mean, so there's tension there all the time, offering benefits people want and offering good service, and each plan and its customers go through this dance, if you will, in the open season, and people make decisions on the margin. The concern I am—and it's all to the good, OK, because you can find the better—if you want acupuncture, you can find a plan with acupuncture and so on. There's all kinds of good things from this model.

The problem I testified on is that I think we have so attenuated the cost-consciousness parts of it, OK, and you can't—you know, the savings to the employee from choosing a more frugal plan now are so small that a lot of the incentive has gone away, and that's one reason I think we've seen these 10, 12, 15-percent-a-year premiums in the last 5 years. They didn't have to be that high. Even if we were outperforming the private sector, we could have more outperformed it. So that's—that's my thought in answer to your question.

Ms. NORTON. Why are they so close? The competition are producing the same price structure?

Mr. FRANCIS. There's a whole bunch of things going on. For example, one thing that people haven't mentioned, the aging of the Federal work force and the increase in the number of annuitants are huge factors. Older people cost more, a lot more, than younger people, but the issue here really is they can't over the long haul—the FEHBP is based and uses private-sector physicians and hospitals. It can't hugely outperform what's going on in the market out there, but what it can do is be a prudent purchaser, and I think it has been and continues to be a prudent purchaser.

I think Kay James is a great OPM Director, and I think her team, the people, are very able. What I think they don't have are quite enough tools. They need to get them from the Congress, including, for example, the design of the Federal contribution, which should be totally budget-neutral. You know, it doesn't have to hurt anybody. It certainly doesn't have to hurt retirees. You don't want to tie it to overall inflation as opposed to medical inflation or the all-plan average. But those added with a little better design features than this program, I think we could see cost increases reduced significantly, you know, back to down to the single-digit levels.

Mr. SCANDLEN. If I could add another important point, one of the things that FEHBP does better than anything else on this is—is transparency and information. Federal workers have a source of good information about what their choices are, and no one else does that as well. It's partly because of OPM, partly because of Walt Francis and a lot of other—I'm sure the labor unions have a lot to do with it. So—so not only do you have choice, but you have real competition because people can compare their choices effectively, and that's a very powerful tool.

Mr. HARNAGE. I might add, too—how are you doing? You're right, we have to look at statistics very carefully. With the California plan going up 25 percent, we don't know whether that was a change in enrollees, a change in participant status, but we do know that over a longer period of time, it outperformed FEHBP. So sort of like your TSP, you can look at the C fund now and not be encouraged to put any money in it, but if you look at it over an 8-year period, it's outperformed all the other funds.

So we have to be very careful when we're looking at statistics and look at more than just the dollars. I'm convinced that we can do better. I'm convinced that we can lower the cost to the taxpayers without taking away benefits from—from the Federal employees. We've just got to do a better job of administering it.

Ms. NORTON. Thank you very much, Mr. Chairman.

Mr. WELDON. You're welcome.

I think Mr. Davis had one more question he wanted to ask one of the witnesses.

Mr. DAVIS OF ILLINOIS. Yes. Thank you, Mr. Chairman.

Mr. Midgett, how do you respond to the less than enthusiastic response to the APWU's plan?

Mr. MIDGETT. Yes, sir, Mr. Davis. For the record, the American Postal Workers Union is opposed to medical savings accounts. We do not believe that the consumer-driven option that we've proposed for benefit year 2003 is a medical savings account. Our option provides 100 percent coverage in network for preventative care. You get the personal care account that you can use for the health care. You have a member responsibility, and you have a traditional PPO product that has catastrophic coverage. To compare our product with the medical savings account, they just—you can't. They're not like one another. I don't know. Mr. Showalter may want to provide additional information.

Mr. SHOWALTER. Thank you.

I think I hear a lot of concerns, and I certainly would never want to leave retirees twisting in the wind also, and I think my mom and dad may disown me if I did such a thing. My mother recently was in an accident in Texas where she spends the winter—I'm from Minneapolis—and under her current medical care plan, she couldn't get treated there. She got treated for an emergency and now has a scarred face, dental work that she cannot get care for in Texas, that she would have to come back up to Minneapolis. Unfortunately my dad has MS, so she can't really come back to Minneapolis to get the medical care she needs because she needs to take care of him. That's the current kind of situation we live under.

So what we really wanted to do was allow people to get in charge of their own medical decisions, not have a managed care company telling people where to get care, how to get care; so we've removed those barriers. In response, there is concerns, and I hear your concerns.

We at Definity Health have been fortunate to have had products in the marketplace for 2½ years that show the concerns aren't coming true, and I really would, you know, congratulate Representative Hoyer on saying there are concerns, but let's take a look at it and see if there can be another solution that really puts patients and doctors back in charge of health care.

And the reason I say that is simply this: Of the plans we're offering to, the average age of the people enrolled in our plans is 41 years old; the average age of the people that they were offered to was about 39 years old. So what happened is people actually—older people that it was offered to actually selected our plan. The average family size in our plans is about 2.6, which means more families chose our plans than single plans, and you might say, hmm, why is this phenomena? And when you think about managed care's value proposition, and we all try to think about new options in a framework of what we're currently underseeing like managed care, in that framework their value proposition was lower cost for less choice—we're going to restrict the provider payment networks and give you less choice, and we're going to increase how much we manage your care. That value proposition is only exciting to people who don't need care. If you don't need care, you don't care how much oversight you have and that you can only go to one hospital.

Our value proposition is go to the providers you want, get the care you need, and be in charge of your own care. The people that value proposition resonates with are the people who experience care in the health care system. Those people are the ones that attenuate to this plan and say, yes, something needs to change. Frankly, no one healthy has enrolled in great numbers in our plan because they don't care. On average they spend less than 7 minutes a year thinking about benefits in total, and health care might be 4 minutes of that. So they don't care. They have not experienced health care. They don't think there's a problem, and if they do, they think it's somebody else's problem.

So I was trying to respond with—I really hear your concern, but I'm trying to respond with the facts as we've experienced them in the private sector.

Mr. DAVIS OF ILLINOIS. Mr. Chairman, I certainly want to thank you for holding this hearing. I want to thank all of the witnesses for coming to testify. The more I hear when we discuss the whole range of possibilities and we look at this business of trying to provide health care, I'm more convinced every time I go through one of these that there's only one way to do it, and that's with a national health plan. So I want to thank you very much. I certainly want to thank all of the witnesses for coming to testify.

Mr. WELDON. You're welcome. I, too, want to thank all our witnesses. I think this has been a most informative hearing. I would ask Members who wish to submit written questions for the record to give them to the subcommittee staff by Friday.

I will leave the record open until December 28th for witnesses to submit their written responses.

The hearing is now adjourned. Again, thank you very much.

[Whereupon, at 2:25 p.m., the subcommittee was adjourned.]

○